W. Root

Silver Up To Date

W. Root

Silver Up To Date

ISBN/EAN: 9783742842596

Manufactured in Europe, USA, Canada, Australia, Japa

Cover: Foto ©Andreas Hilbeck / pixelio.de

Manufactured and distributed by brebook publishing software (www.brebook.com)

W. Root

Silver Up To Date

UP TO DATE

BY

W. ROOT

LONDON:
GEORGE PHILIP & SON, 32 FLEET STREET, E.C.
LIVERPOOL: 45 TO 51 SOUTH CASTLE STREET.
1894.

PREFACE.

It is an ill wind that blows nobody any good, and however severely the depreciation of silver may have told upon the community generally, it has benefitted at least three classes of it—printers, ink manufacturers, and papermakers. Whether those responsible for the great mass of literature published on the subject are to be regarded as public benefactors or public nuisances, it is not for me to say. If I am placed in the latter category, my excuse for inflicting this little volume upon my readers must be, that just prior to the Brussels Conference I published a pamphlet dealing with the subject, which was received with marked favour both by the press and in private circles; and, in view of its growing importance, I have ventured to write a somewhat larger work, in which, however, what was best in the original has been incorporated. I have purposely avoided the use of any elaborate statistics, which it is truly said can be made to prove anything, and have even kept clear as far as possible of the simplest figures. It has been my object to write a short history of the entire difficulty in as concise and simple a manner as possible, and with the view of bringing the facts home to everybody, whether they have previously studied the question or not.

Like most other writers on the subject, I have ventured to propound a remedy. It is only human nature to believe that one's own geese are always swans; I will not insult mine by venturing to suggest that they may only be lame ducks. I must leave the public to decide whether my proposal is a feasible one. It may be difficult of accomplishment, and involve some risk, but in these respects it differs nothing from any of its competitors. One merit I do claim for it—that it will not interfere with the real market value of silver, and that, placing the metal in no artificial position, there need never be any fear of a disastrous collapse.

Liverpool, April, 1804.   J. W. R.

CONTENTS.

PTER	I.—THE ORIGIN OF THE SILVER QUESTION	7
,,	II.—SOME RESULTS OF THE DEPRECIATION OF SILVER	14
,,	III.—THE LANCASHIRE COTTON TRADE	24
,,	IV.—SILVER LEGISLATION IN THE UNITED STATES	31
,,	V.—THE CLOSING OF THE INDIAN MINTS	45
,,	VI.—REMEDIES: NATURAL AND ARTIFICIAL	61
,,	VII.—BIMETALLISM	74
,,	VIII.—CLASS INTERESTS AND THE SILVER QUESTION	89
,,	IX.—A NEW OUTLET FOR SILVER	100
,,	X.—SILVER AND THE LABOUR QUESTION	118

Chapter I.

THE ORIGIN OF THE SILVER QUESTION.

All the best known writers on Political Economy have treated of the nature and functions of money. Without examining their theories very closely, it will nevertheless be just as well to start with some clear understanding as to what money, as represented by gold and silver, either coined or in the form of bullion, really is, particularly as an idea seems to be prevalent that there is something approaching a halo of sanctity surrounding these two precious metals.

Put very briefly, money is simply a commodity, which is readily accepted in every part of the civilised world in exchange for any other commodity. In its simple form of bullion, it must be carefully weighed and assayed before it can meet with such acceptance, and to save time as well as trouble, therefore, the various Governments of the world have affixed their stamp upon pieces of gold and silver, which is a full guarantee both as to their weight and quality. Gold and silver as such are amongst the most useless metals, but their comparative scarceness and cost of extraction have given them from the remotest ages an artificial value for purposes of exchange, and even their use as ornaments is based largely upon their ready conversion into the necessaries of life.

Gold and silver have therefore become the world's money, simply because of all known commodities they have been found to possess the most favourable properties. Indestructible with ordinary usage, and at the same time lending themselves readily to the manipulation of the tools of the mint or the workshop; sufficiently scarce to make them costly compared with almost every other article of nature's production, and yet plentiful enough to fulfil the main function required of them, namely, to be the standards by which all other commodities may be measured or valued. It is well known that some of the African tribes use small shells for monetary purposes, but whatever value they possess is confined to their own territories; beyond them they become valueless. In the same way there would be no absolute reason why all the nations of the earth should not meet together in congress, and decide that in future some other commodities—say, for instance, palm kernels or pea nuts—should become the medium of exchange for all other commodities. What makes any such suggestion preposterous and absolutely impossible of application, quite apart from the natural resistance with which it would meet from the owners of the world's gold and silver, would be the fact that no other commodity is at present known which would adequately fulfil in all its qualities the eminently suitable ones of these two metals.

Sufficient has been said to show that the position gold and silver occupy in the world's trade and commerce is largely due to sentimental as well as practical reasons, and that, even if scientific discovery revealed some other commodity in many respects more suitable for the purposes of universal exchange, vested interests would prove too strong to permit of any change being made. It becomes necessary, then, to consider their relation to one another, and to discover the causes which have led, by the appreciation of the one and the depreciation of the other, to the present disastrous depression which has overtaken the world's commerce.

Although both metals have from time immemorial been used for monetary and exchange purposes, silver was until the present century the universal and single standard of value, upon which all trade was conducted, and wherever gold was made use of, it was in some fixed but by no means unvarying proportion of its value to silver. Gold coins issued from the mint were simply token money, just as our silver coins are to-day. Gold bullion was shipped from one country to another in settlement of trade balances, and credited to the account of the shipper for its value in the silver money of the country. The first nation to make a change in this respect was England, and that owing to accident, and not to design.

Everyone who has read Lord Macaulay's inimitable *History of England* will remember his graphic account of the inconveniences, losses, and sufferings occasioned by the debased and clipped silver coinage which passed as money prior to and during the reign of William III. and Mary. The financial reformers of that age, headed by Montagu, worked out and adopted, in the year 1696, a scheme for placing the currency on a sound basis, and by severe penal laws protecting it from fraud. One item of the programme was the coinage of the golden guinea, nominally to represent twenty-one shillings, but which actually contained the value of twenty-one shillings and sixpence worth of the current English silver. The money dealers of Lombard Street soon discovered this mistake, and found that by sending twenty-one shillings of silver abroad they could purchase sufficient gold to coin a guinea, and have a little over for profit. In this way the silver coinage of the country began rapidly to disappear, until at the instance of Sir Isaac Newton, a great economist, as well as a great philosopher, the value of the guinea was reduced to twenty-one shillings. Even this was too high, the exact value should have been only twenty

The Origin of the Silver Question

shillings and eightpence, and the transaction, although less profitable, still continued to be carried on to a moderate extent. Silver now came to be used only in small quantities, and the guinea became the current coin of the realm; but it was not until the year 1816, or one hundred and twenty years later, that Parliament finally recognised it as the unit of value, and so established for the first time the single gold standard.

But for this accident, therefore, the currency of not only England, but all Europe, might to-day have been based on a silver standard, and gold been simply commercial or token money. Of course other circumstances have arisen during the present century which might have effected the change, notably the great gold discoveries in California and Australia, which in a few years doubled the world's supply of the precious metal, but this is too indefinite a point, and hardly worth discussing.

For more than half a century after this England remained the solitary instance of a nation whose currency was based upon a gold standard. Every other country maintained the silver basis to which the world was accustomed, coining gold as token money, when required, in some fixed ratio to silver.

The Silver question, as it is now known to us, may be said to have first made its appearance about the year 1873. Prior to that period silver had been for a long time steadily maintained in value at about 60d. per ounce; the value of the Indian rupee was regarded as fixed at two shillings; the Mints of Europe, except the English, were open to coin silver and gold to all comers in the proportion of 15½ to 1, and the circulating medium was a silver coinage. At the conclusion of the Franco-Prussian war, however, the victorious Germans decided that the enormous indemnity imposed upon France should be made use of for the extension of German trade and commerce; and, anxious to profit as much as possible by the past experience of England, arrived at the conclusion that the first step must be the establishment of a gold basis for their currency. The silver thaler must make way for the golden mark, and as fast as the German Treasury could accumulate gold, it endeavoured to dispose of equal quantities of its silver coinage. But Europe soon refused to take any more of the thalers at their face value, and only for the market value of the metal they contained—in fact, the old currency of Germany was no longer regarded as money, but simply as metal. The forced sale of such large quantities slowly but surely broke down the value, and, with one or two slight reactions of short duration, it has been declining ever since.

The floods of silver poured out from Germany to be exchanged for gold, threatened to deplete the stocks of gold of every other nation whose Mints were open to the coinage of silver, and it was to prevent this that the French and other continental governments declined any longer to exchange their gold for silver, and coin it for the public at any ratio whatever.

Such was the commencement of the demonetisation of silver, and, as is well known, the silver coins current in this and other European countries are merely tokens, worth now intrinsically considerably less than half their face value, and legally tenderable in discharge of debt to only a limited amount. This suspension of silver coinage by the nations forming the Latin Union has for all practical purposes converted them into gold standard countries, as it is the knowledge that the silver currency will not be increased in quantity which permits it to circulate freely at its face value. Quite recently Austria-Hungary has fallen into line with her Western neighbours, and has absorbed large quantities of gold for the purpose of consolidating her gold standard. Only Russia and Turkey amongst European nations have not adopted it; the former, as much an Asiatic as a European Power, still maintains an inconvertible paper based upon silver; the latter, if its currency can be said to have a name at all, is cosmopolitan.

Chapter II.

SOME RESULTS OF THE DEPRECIATION OF SILVER.

Various interests were gradually awakened to the fact that some great change was in progress. The large and growing commerce between England and the East, more particularly India and China, was for the first time feeling the effects of fluctuating exchanges; and whereas in former times almost the only questions a merchant or shipper had to take into account were those of supply and demand, the most important one was fast becoming—How many rupees or taels he would receive for the sovereign? Twenty years ago he knew to a certainty that when his goods were sold in India for ten rupees, whether it was one month hence or six, he would receive for those ten rupees a pound sterling. Of late years it has been impossible to foretell whether, when his shipments were realised, the ten rupees would bring him in fifteen shillings, or fourteen, or even less, in accordance with the price at which silver or exchange might then be standing. Trade with the East, therefore, is now attended with risks formerly unknown, and the method of carrying it on has had to undergo serious modifications. The great consignments of Manchester and other goods sent out by manufacturers and shippers are no longer possible, as the fluctuations in exchange even during the voyage might be so great as to involve in a considerable loss what would otherwise have proved a profitable transaction. The native dealers and merchants are now generally called upon to take this risk, and by transmitting to this country the orders for what they may require, the English shipper is enabled to at once conclude an arrangement with one of the great Eastern Banks as to the rate of exchange. The effects of this change are frequently visible in Lancashire, for while in former days manufacturers would ship to the East all the calico they could make, and never dream of stopping their machinery, now, if orders from India or China are scarce, large numbers of looms are invariably at rest, and consequently, many hands out of employment.

But, after all, these effects are of a very trivial nature compared with those devolving upon other interested classes of the community, for it is the *fluctuations* in the value of silver or in the rate of exchange which trouble the English shipper, and were a fixed value to be universally agreed upon for that metal, it would be of small consequence to him whether it was 30d. or 60d. an ounce. But to the Indian Government, the official classes, and the great financial institutions engaged in the trade between Europe or America and the East, the consequences of the decline in silver were most disastrous. A large portion of the annual expenditure of the Indian Government has to be made in this country, consisting of interest on the loans raised here from time to time, payments made on account of wages, salaries, and pensions to soldiers, officers, and others in the employ of Government, and payments for whatever supplies may be needed. In round figures, some £15,000,000 is annually due on balance by the Indian Government to the English, and has in some way to be provided for. This is done by the India Council in London selling bills upon the Treasuries of Calcutta, Bombay, and Madras, generally to the banks engaged in the Eastern trade, who remit them to their agencies in India in payment of the mercantile bills drawn against shipments of produce, and bought by these agencies, who in turn remit them to London. Were silver at its old price of 60d. per ounce and exchange at two shillings the rupee, the Indian Government would be called upon to provide annually, say, 150,000,000 rupees; but with exchange at only one shilling and twopence, that payment is raised to 250,000,000, or a direct loss of 100,000,000 rupees, equal to nearly £6,000,000, at the present exchange. This loss the Indian Government must either make good by increased taxation, or borrow to make up the deficit; and it was no wonder, therefore, that Indian officials regarded with dismay the continued depreciation of silver, when every penny decline taxed them to the extent of something approaching £1,000,000, and with the burdens laid upon the natives already quite as great as they could bear, and further taxation dangerous.

The fall also told with great severity upon the large class of officials who received their salaries and pensions in the native currency. So long as they remained in India the hardship was felt but slightly, if at all, but if compelled to send remittances home for the education and support of any portion of their families, or returning themselves after their period of service had expired, they at once found their allowances very materially reduced. Fifteen or twenty years ago an annual salary of 15,000 rupees, and perhaps a retiring pension of half the amount, would prove a strong attraction to many who would look forward to spending the later years of their life amidst their old friends and associations, counting on an income of £750 per annum. But while the 7,500 rupees remain, the £750 has gradually dwindled away to something under £500, and where pensions have been small and proportionately reduced, much distress and suffering have no doubt ensued.

For the same reasons most of the Eastern banks and financial institutions located in Europe have also suffered heavy losses. Their capital and deposits are largely raised in this country in gold, much of which has been exchanged into silver and remitted abroad for trading and ordinary banking purposes, and if returned now and re-exchanged into gold would leave a serious deficiency. One institution entirely collapsed owing to losses incurred largely from this cause, another had to undergo the process of reconstruction, while most others are known to have been more or less weakened.

It is little to be wondered at that the complaints from all parts of our Eastern possessions, and from those connected with them, should have been loud and long, and that they demanded that some measures should be adopted, or at any rate attempted, to stem the current of depreciation; and it was no doubt principally in deference to these expressions of opinion that the English Government consented to be represented at the Brussels Conference held in 1892. At the same time it would be a mistake to suppose that the fall in silver has been prejudicial to the native population of India. Indeed, it cannot be disputed that on the whole they are wealthier and generally in more comfortable circumstances than twenty years ago, when silver was double its present price. The rupee, the anna, and the pice are to them quite as valuable to-day as they were then, and purchase the same equivalent, while they undoubtedly possess more of them; and nothing would astonish an Indian ryot more than to be informed that the value of money during that period had undergone a serious change. For while the value of the rupee has been undergoing a serious diminution from the European standpoint, the value of the commodities dealt in by the natives has undergone a corresponding change, and the one has counteracted the other. The wheat, the linseed, the cotton which he has to sell have fallen enormously in value in the Western world, but the quarter of wheat which sold perhaps at 45s. when the rupee was 2s., and for which he received $22\frac{1}{2}$ rupees, now brings him $21\frac{1}{2}$ rupees when the rupee is at 1s. 2d., although actually sold for only 25s., and from his standpoint, at least, wheat may possibly be worth more at 25s. than it was at 45s. On the other hand, he might be expected to have to pay more for his clothes, salt, and other necessaries of life, but the decline in the sterling values of these articles has been so great that even when converted into the depreciated rupee he pays no more for them than formerly. The only point where the shoe is likely to pinch is the increased taxation which Government may be compelled to impose, to make good the serious loss in Exchange already referred to.

True, a check has been imposed upon the construction of railways and other great public works requiring the help of European capital. Investors will no longer subscribe to such undertakings in face of the serious risk of a further decline in exchange, and of the silver which would have to be shipped to carry them out being returned to them in years to come at a depreciated price, nor does the Indian Government feel itself justified in giving any more guarantees. But this does not involve any great annual amount, and is, after all, only a temporary matter, as sooner or later silver must stop declining, with the probability that the accumulation of much necessary but delayed work will prove a great stimulus to trade.

While the changes going on have had but little effect on the agricultural producers of the Eastern, they have been working a revolution among those of the Western world, more particularly the farmers and planters of the United States. So long as the Eastern grower is content to accept the same number of rupees for his produce as in former days, and the value of that rupee, or of silver, continues to decline, so long will the European importer be enabled to sell at continually declining prices, and the wheat and cotton so largely produced in India come into competition with the same productions from Europe and America, and force down the prices of the latter as well.

No doubt machinery, fertilizers, and improved methods of production and transport, have had something to do with the slow but continuous and now heavy decline in most articles of agricultural produce, but careful examination will show that those largely or almost exclusively grown in silver-using countries have suffered the most. Thus Wheat and Cotton, both of which are grown very largely in India, are at, or very close to, the lowest prices ever recorded. Rice and Tea, for which we are dependent almost entirely on Eastern countries, are at prices which would a few years ago have been ridiculed as beyond the chance of possibility. Sugar and Coffee, on the other hand, which are not largely produced in silver-using countries, stand considerably above lowest record prices, although it cannot be supposed that so general a decline as we have witnessed of late years has not affected most articles of commerce, irrespective of intrinsic values. It is perfectly evident, therefore, that the depreciation of silver must have exercised an enormous influence on the fall in prices, and consequent trade depression.

Nor are the reasons difficult to discover. Governments representing two-thirds of the population of the globe, including, of course, India, where the change to a gold standard is by no means yet an accomplished fact, still adhere to the old-fashioned silver basis. Moreover, they comprise the governments and people least intelligent, of little or no education, and, consequently, the slowest to move. They have been accustomed for generations to sell the produce of their lands for a certain amount of money, and when this is not obtainable they bury their wheat, linseed, or cotton in the earth, until either they get their price or famine and want compel them to realise. Once the price is obtainable they do not argue upon the possibility of getting more, but sell out all they possess. They have been equally accustomed to pay definite prices for the articles of clothing and other necessaries they are compelled to purchase. When they get them on these terms the demand is steady and normal. They ask for no reduction, but equally insist on paying no advance, or if compelled to do so, and unable absolutely to go without, reduce their wants to a minimum. Against this solid conservative mass of two-thirds of the world's inhabitants has been pitted the remaining third, quick in intelligence, steady in progress, and able rapidly to adapt itself to changed circumstances. It is not to be wondered at, therefore, that the Western World, impatient at the slowness of the Eastern to comprehend the necessity of an adjustment of values, has itself been the first to give way, and so, paradoxical though it may appear, throw the great losses involved in the depreciation of silver upon the gold standard nations.

The effects have naturally been felt far beyond the range of agricultural producers. It is a mere truism that anything which affects agriculture must tell sooner or later upon all other trades and industries, the prosperity or depression of the one reflecting itself upon the other. In the case of manufacturers depending largely upon Eastern custom, the same depressing influences have been at work which have proved so injurious to agriculture, and more than one great branch of industry has felt the severity of the crisis.

Chapter III.

THE LANCASHIRE COTTON TRADE.

The Lancashire Cotton Trade has always regarded our Indian dependencies as their best customers, and has viewed with alarm the growing and prosperous condition of the cotton spinning and manufacturing industry in Bombay. Manchester succeeded some years ago in obtaining the abolition of the duties on imported cotton goods into India, which gave a small advantage to the native producer, and has just successfully resisted their re-imposition. Rightly or wrongly, Manchester shippers believe that every decline in the value of the rupee gives their Indian competitor a fresh advantage, and, on precisely the same grounds as they agitated for the removal of the duties, now demand that Government shall take steps to prevent any further depreciation in the exchange. That many of them are sincere in their belief that the adoption of bimetallism would bring other advantages in its train there can be little doubt, but once remove the particular grievance from which they themselves suffer, and they would probably not think the agitation worth carrying on. It is argued that every time silver declines, Manchester has to take less for its shirtings and calicoes, while the rupee being the standard of value in the East, the Bombay manufacturer has to submit to no such decline, and therefore obtains an undue advantage. But it is forgotten that a decline in silver is almost invariably accompanied by a decline in raw cotton, which reduces the cost of the Lancashire production, while frequently no corresponding decline takes place in the raw material in Bombay, for the simple reason that the Liverpool importer can afford to pay the same number of rupees, and yet, owing to the exchange, sell at a lower sterling price. Owing to the impossibility of calculating and providing against every little change, undoubtedly there is at times some disadvantage of the sort, but it is frequently more than compensated in other directions. The Lancashire manufacturer has many customers at home and abroad who are not affected by fluctuations in silver, and the fall in the metal, while frequently enabling him to purchase his raw material on better terms, does not compel him to make a corresponding reduction in the price of his production.

A little examination, too, will prove their contention to be entirely fallacious, and although the price of cotton goods has been no exception to the general depression, the real causes of native competition must be sought elsewhere. In the first place, it must be remembered that India is a large cotton producing country. The quality of the growth may be much inferior to that of any other, and it can only be used for the production of an inferior class of goods, but these are largely in demand in the East. Up to about the year 1880 the cotton spinning industry in India was conducted on a very moderate scale, but within the past fourteen years the number of mills and spindles has more than doubled. Up to the former period the bulk of the cotton was shipped to Europe, manufactured here and returned to the East for sale. But British capital and British enterprise in India have gradually devised means of saving the great cost of transit and all the various charges and commissions involved, until now nearly the whole of the trade in the coarser and cheaper goods has been lost to Lancashire. That this has occurred during a period of decline in the value of silver is a coincidence rather than an explanation. It is perfectly natural that any country producing the raw material, possessed of ample capital, natural facilities, and cheap labour, must sooner or later compete successfully with a country which is thousands of miles away from the sources of production, and this is exactly what has happened to India. Freights to and from Bombay, Liverpool charges and commissions, inland transit and numerous other items, really form a bounty to the

Indian mill-owner; and it is a marvellous proof of the vitality and soundness of British trade, that, with all these advantages and ridiculously cheap labour thrown in, he is only just able to compete successfully with his Lancashire rival. There has been a great deal of talk the past year or two of the manufacture in India of fine goods made from American cotton, but the few thousand bales annually exported to our Eastern possession amount to nothing, and is less than the quantity used by many a first-class English spinner. The relative quality and coarseness of the yarn spun in the two countries may be gathered from the fact, that while the average consumption of American cotton spun in England is about sixteen ounces per week to the spindle, in India it is no less than forty, and while the hours of work in the latter instance are longer, it is certain the inferior labour does not produce any greater results. Unless totally unforeseen circumstances arise, whatever the course of exchange may be, this country has but little to fear from the competition of India in the production of fine goods, which, as the East advances in prosperity, will come more and more into demand.

But it is pointed out that whenever silver declines the Manchester shipper must either raise his price to the Indian consumer, or accept a lower price here, as the same number of rupees will only exchange for a lower sterling value, and that, consequently, the Indian manufacturer derives an undue benefit, by being able to produce at the same cost as before, while under no necessity to advance his prices. A little enquiry, however, will show any such advantage to be purely visionary, except, perhaps, just at the moment when a change in silver occurs. In the month of July, 1890, for instance, when silver was in the neighbourhood of 50d. per ounce, good Oomrawuttee cotton, and fully good fair Dhollerah cotton, both standard qualities of growths largely consumed by Bombay mills, were quoted respectively in the Bombay market at 195 and 193 rupees per candy, while middling American cotton was quoted in Liverpool at the same time at $6\frac{9}{16}$d. per pound. In the month of August, 1892, the same growths were quoted in Bombay at 178 and 180 rupees per candy respectively, while middling American cotton stood in Liverpool at $3\frac{15}{16}$d. per pound, and silver was worth only about $38\frac{1}{2}$d. per ounce. A month later prices in Bombay showed little change, while middling American had risen in Liverpool to $4\frac{1}{4}$d. Now, it will be seen that, compared with July, 1890, the Bombay cotton spinner purchased his raw material in August, 1892, at a decline of 13 to 17 rupees per candy, or something less than 10 per cent., while the Lancashire spinner purchased his at a decline of $2\frac{5}{8}$d. per pound, or exactly 40 per cent. If the month of September be taken, the decline was only $2\frac{5}{16}$d. per pound, or a little over 35 per cent. But the 40 per cent. does not represent the full advantage obtained by the Lancashire mill-owner, as not only does the reduced cost permit the employment of reduced capital, and consequently a saving of interest paid, probably, to some bank or broker for overdraft or advance, but the waste always entailed in converting cotton into yarn has cost him only $3\frac{15}{16}$d. per pound, instead of $6\frac{9}{16}$d. It is evident, therefore, that the Lancashire spinner had bought his cotton at least 25 to 30 per cent. cheaper than his Indian competitor, while in the same period silver had declined barely the lower per centage. Even allowing for the fact that wages and fixed charges show little, if any, decline within the same period, the disadvantage, if there be any at all, can be but very slight.

The examples given have been chosen as representing extreme prices in the value of raw cotton, and not because they show any specially favourable result. They could be multiplied indefinitely, and would undoubtedly show variations both ways, but the broad fact remains, that a decline or advance in silver is promptly compensated by a relative change in the value of the raw material between Bombay and Liverpool. A steady rate of exchange between England and the East would undoubtedly, in many instances, facilitate business, but whether the rate is a high or low one is of little consequence.

The effects of silver depreciation are sufficiently serious without laying at its door any for which it is not really responsible, and were Lancashire to have her way, and, by the introduction of bimetallism, raise the price of silver and of Indian exchange to something like the former level, she would find she had not greatly mended matters as far as native competition was concerned. Besides, we have not yet arrived at the point where India is to be governed for the benefit of Lancashire, and the ideas prevalent in the days of the old East India Company have gone, let us hope, for ever. If, without the unnatural forcing of protective duties, India can establish and maintain a great cotton manufacturing industry, it would be criminal on the part of the British Government to attempt to destroy it. All Lancashire can ask for—and she has got it—is fairplay.

Chapter IV.

SILVER LEGISLATION IN THE UNITED STATES.

Among the first to suffer from the depreciation of silver were, of course, the mine-owners and producers of the metal, who witnessed their output gradually diminishing in value, and were naturally anxious to do something to put a stop to the decline. The United States and Mexico being by far the largest producers, it was in these countries where the pinch was most severely felt; and as the European Governments had now closed their mints against any further public coinage of silver, efforts were made to induce or compel that of the United States to open theirs. The silver interest, which was possessed of great wealth, and consequently of much political influence, at length succeeded in passing through Congress, in the year 1878, what is known as the Bland Act, which was an Act compelling the Secretary of the Treasury of the United States to buy every month sufficient silver to coin at least two, and not more than four, million silver dollars. The expectation was that these silver dollars would obtain a wide circulation throughout the States —an expectation completely falsified, as the vast bulk of them still lie in the vaults of the Treasury, although they are represented to some extent by the notes issued and circulating against them. But even this measure only imposed a temporary check on the decline.

Agitation was once more stimulated, and the Silver interest in the States made the most of the depressed and continuously declining prices from which the farmers were beginning to suffer, forced home upon them to what a large extent this was due to the depreciation of the white metal, and urged upon them the necessity of rehabilitating silver if they wished to obtain improved prices for their produce. This was no doubt at the bottom of the agitation which was carried on there for several years, which split up both political parties, and assumed a contest of the Eastern against the Western and Southern States. The bait took so well that still greater advantages were held out than even the improvement in the value of their produce. It was urged that if the currency were largely increased by the addition of silver, the fact of so much money circulating throughout the country would still further tend to raise prices, and it was also pointed out that the mortgages and loans due by the farmers to Eastern bankers and capitalists could be discharged on much more favourable terms were silver to be declared legal tender to any amount. The agitation proved so successful that in 1890 the Silver party in Congress was so strong as to be able to repeal the Bland Act, and pass one of a much more drastic and wide-reaching character—since known as the Sherman Act. By it the Secretary to the Treasury was compelled to purchase, not two and a half million dollars, upon which basis the Bland Act had been worked, but four and a half million ounces of silver per month, at the market price of the day, which was to be deposited in the Treasury vaults, and certificates for its value issued against it, which should be legal tender to any amount through the length and breadth of the land. Thus was stopped the coinage of the two and a half million standard silver dollars, which it had long become impossible to force into circulation, and substituted for it a measure compelling the purchase of four and a half million ounces, against which certificates should be issued payable in either gold or silver; and, so long as the United States Government remains solvent, equally as good as our Bank of England notes. The total of such certificates issued under this Act amounted to nearly one hundred and fifty million dollars, or close upon £30,000,000, which the Treasury was liable to be called upon for payment in gold, and which, as a matter of fact, has never been refused for any portion so far presented.

Whatever might be its ultimate effect upon the finances of the United States, it was confidently anticipated that silver, which before the agitation commenced was in the neighbourhood of 43d. or 44d. per ounce, would experience an immense rise in price. Nor was this anticipation ill-founded. Long before the Act was passed an immense speculation sprang up, and capitalists and syndicates laid in great stocks of the metal, while all stocks and shares based upon silver went up by leaps and bounds. Abandoned mines, which no longer paid at the depreciated prices, were restarted, and activity reigned everywhere. The Eastern Banks anticipated their future requirements of the precious metal, and even the English Government purchased largely, with a view of increasing the silver currency, and displacing to some extent the expensive half sovereign. The speculation extended largely to cotton and other articles of produce, and for a time it seemed as though the financial and commercial millennium had arrived. The sudden additional demand for about twenty-five million ounces of silver per annum was calculated to create a veritable scarcity, and many sanguine persons believed the price would speedily reach what was regarded as par, or 60d. per ounce.

The final passage of the Act culminated the excitement, and for a short time silver was quoted at 54d. But it was soon discovered that other and unseen causes had also been at work. It was known that several of the European Governments, notably that of Germany, still held large stocks of the metal, of which they were only awaiting a favourable opportunity to dispose. Whether they did so, and to what extent, remains a secret; but it is well known that the Roumanian Government sold a large quantity in Vienna at a high price with a view to extending their gold currency. Rich silver mines were about the same time being opened up in Australia, and the high prices caused operations to be urged forward, with the result that one of the mines, the Broken Hill Proprietary Company, reached an output at the rate of ten million ounces per annum—no small addition to the production of the world; while it is claimed there are other mines in the neighbourhood which will eventually prove equally rich. The speculators and syndicates, seeing no further rise in prices, became uneasy, and one after another began to liquidate their holdings. To crown all, the Eastern financial institutions, which had already to some extent anticipated their future requirements, found themselves suddenly confronted with a famine in India, and the greatly reduced exports from that country materially diminished the requirements for remittances thither.

It was not to be wondered at that the increased output from the mines and the sudden appearance of old stocks of the metal, combined with the lessened demand from the regular sources, should more than counterbalance the increased purchases of the United States Government, and that the price would consequently decline instead of advance. This was exactly what happened, and although a few people foresaw this probability at the time, no one dreamt that the value of the metal would sink so quickly much below anything previously recorded. The pendulum was swung too far in one direction, and is now probably reacting too far in the other.

Once more an endeavour was made to stem the decline by fresh legislation. This time it was a Free Coinage Bill—in other words, anyone was to be at liberty to lodge silver with the Treasury to an unlimited extent, and demand that it should be coined into dollars of a certain fixed weight and fineness, and by this means it was hoped to set a definite and fixed value upon the metal itself. But the experience of the Sherman Act opened the eyes of many people to the extreme danger of even the then limited accumulation. Upwards of fifty million dollars in gold had been shipped to Europe; the certificates issued against the monthly purchases were continually being presented to the Treasury, and paid in gold; and that institution, whose reserves a few years before had been the wonder and envy of every nation in Europe, now began to find itself in the position of holding its reserve in the form of certificates issued against silver, and its stock of gold below the amount required by law to provide for the gold certificates and greenbacks in circulation throughout the country. It was clearly foreseen that at no distant period the Treasury must decline to pay in gold, or increase its liabilities by issuing a gold loan wherewith to replenish its almost empty coffers. It was quite true the Secretary could pay the certificates issued against silver bullion in silver coin, but the moment he insisted on doing so, gold would go to a premium. Precautions began to be taken with a view to such an eventuality, and all loans contracted, and many ordinary mercantile operations entered into, were expressly provided for to be liquidated in *gold*, as against any mere legal tender money. Bankers throughout the States accumulated stocks of the precious metal, many of them at the expense of the Treasury, and took care to make their payments in legal tender notes, while carefully hoarding the gold. It seemed certain that one of two things must shortly happen—either that the currency of the United States must descend to a silver basis, or that the purchases of silver and consequent issue of legal tender notes payable in gold must be altogether suspended. It was the fear of the latter event which brought about a semi-panic and forced silver down to 38d. per ounce; and the question was naturally asked to what price it might go if an additional four and a half million ounces over and above the existing supplies were to be forced upon the market every month.

Such was the state of affairs when, in November, 1892, the people of the United States were called upon to elect a new President. The then existing Government of President Harrison had distinguished itself not only by the silver legislation of 1890, but also by the passage of the M'Kinley Tariff, and both measures combined had already begun to tell upon the general prosperity of the country. Mr. Cleveland boldly appealed to the electors as a determined opponent of the M'Kinley Tariff, as well as the Sherman Silver Act, and promised, if elected, a prompt repeal at anyrate of the latter. Judging by the result, the eyes of the country must have been widely opened to the dangers which threatened, and despite all the persuasion of the silver party, a vastly preponderating vote was cast in favour of sound currency. Notwithstanding Mr. Cleveland's victory, and his determination to lose no time in bringing about some radical change—as shown by the calling of a special Session of Congress—confidence was not restored, as doubts were entertained whether the new President's party in either the House of Representatives or the Senate would prove sufficiently strong to carry a Repeal Act;

and the summer of 1893 proved one of the most disastrous periods known in the history of the United States. For a short time gold was at a premium over the regular currency, while banks as well as large mercantile and trading concerns suspended payment all over the country, owing to the scarcity of currency, brought about by hoarding and the enormous shipments of gold to Europe; while even the New York banks were compelled to adopt the expedient of a large issue of clearing-house certificates to prevent some of them closing their doors.

The decision come to upon the question by the House of Representatives was prompt as well as unexpectedly decisive, and it was hoped would convince the Senate of the advisability, if not indeed the necessity, of acting in a similar spirit. Any expectation of this sort, however, was doomed to be disappointed; and the contest over the Repeal Act, in the Upper House, is likely to become historical in the annals of Parliamentary Government. The Repealers supporting President Cleveland were believed to be in a small—but only a small—majority; and all the arts of Parliamentary obstruction were called into play by the Silver party to defeat the measure. It had always been imagined that obstruction had reached its acme of perfection in the British House of Commons, but in this respect, as in most others, Brother Jonathan proved he could go one better. Unaccustomed to such tactics, the rules of the Senate had been framed in a way to lend themselves easily to the manipulation of any large minority determined upon resisting the will of the majority. It was open to any Senator to speak as often as he liked and as long as he liked; and it is recorded that, at least in one instance, a speech was delivered of fifteen hours' duration! To overcome this resistance, the majority determined upon a continuous sitting until Repeal was passed; but, as for this purpose it was necessary to keep a majority of the Senate always at hand to form a quorum, the Silver men quickly discovered that, by absenting themselves and insisting upon a quorum being continually present, they could tax the physical powers of their opponents beyond endurance; and although the latter had arranged to live altogether within the precincts of their building, they found that the vigilance of the opposite party prevented them obtaining sleep, or indeed rest of any sort.

The contest proved too severe, and had to be given up; and it was felt throughout the United States, as well as Europe, that the Repeal party was defeated, and that the most the President could hope for was a compromise, in which the continued purchase of silver would be limited to a definite number of years. But he proved himself more determined than even his warmest admirers could have imagined; and, supported by the conviction that the voice of the country was calling loudly for the measure, and that until it was passed there could be no hope of a return to commercial prosperity, he succeeded by dogged perseverance in overthrowing every obstacle and forcing the question to a vote, when, by a small but sufficient majority, the Sherman Silver Act ceased to be law. Needless to say, he did not lose a day in giving his assent; since when the Government of the United States has ceased purchasing a single ounce of silver bullion.

It is quite true that the eagerly looked for reaction in trade has not taken place; and America has apparently yet to learn that she cannot act on false economical doctrines without being compelled to suffer for it. But the present stagnation is due largely to other causes, and partly also to the exhaustion following a bitter and at the same time a doubtful conflict. Prior to and during the discussion of the Silver Act, gold was withdrawn from the Treasury by the Banks, and from the Banks by depositors when they could get it; and money became unobtainable on the very best security at any rate of interest. The repeal of the Purchase Act having restored confidence, at any rate, in the currency of the country, the money so withdrawn and hoarded soon found its way back into the Banks; but, in the almost total absence of commercial or manufacturing enterprise, it remains there, and instead of being unobtainable, is now almost unlendable. This want of enterprise is due now, perhaps, more to questions relating to the Tariff than to Silver, but there can be little doubt that while both are responsible for the great crisis through which the country is passing, the latter must bear the larger part of it.

Although deposits flowed rapidly back into the Banks, the Treasury itself was not replenished, and the continued withdrawals of gold had left its holdings at a dangerously, as well as illegally, low level. To repair this a gold loan of fifty million dollars has recently been issued, the subscriptions to which, however, but little exceeded that amount, and came almost entirely from New York Bankers. But it has enabled the Secretary of the Treasury to bring up the gold deposits once more to the hundred million dollars, and has consequently answered the purpose for which it was intended.

Such, then, has been the history of Silver legislation in the United States, and such are its results. Despite their disastrous nature, which might lead one to suppose that the people of that country would in future leave the white metal to take care of itself, the Silver party, so far from being dead, cannot be said to be even slumbering. Their power in both Houses of Congress has just been evinced by the passage of the Bland Seigniorage Bill, a measure of not much importance in itself, but showing that all the elements are in existence for a fresh campaign in favour of silver. The Bill did not increase the quantity of silver in the Treasury, but simply called upon the Secretary to calculate the difference between the actual amount of the certificates issued against the three years' purchases under the Sherman Act, and the nominal value of the silver itself if coined into legal United States dollars, and to at once proceed to coin the difference, whatever it may be, into such legal dollars. This would mean the fresh coinage of at least fifty million dollars, but out of silver already owned by, and in the possession of, the Treasury. As it is extremely unlikely that these coins could ever be forced into circulation, the next proposal would probably be to issue legal tender notes against them, and to once more largely increase the currency of the country, for which, at the present moment at any rate, there is not the slightest need.

There never could have been any question as to the feeling of President Cleveland regarding this Bill, although at one time there were doubts as to whether he might not after all assent to it. Had he done so it would not have been on economical grounds, but rather as a matter of expediency, and to secure support for the Tariff Bill; arguing, no doubt, that as it would not increase the national hoard of silver, its effect could not be particularly baneful. But the pressure of banking and commercial interests, particularly on the part of the subscribers to the recent gold loan, settled the matter, if it was ever in doubt, and the Bill has been, for the time being, rejected by the Presidential veto. It need not be supposed that the last has been heard of it, and although any fresh legislation in the interests of silver is unlikely during the existing administration, it must rest finally with the people of the country to say, through their elected representatives, whether past experience has been sufficient, or whether they are still willing to start out on fresh paths of adventure. It would be idle to attempt to prophesy the answer.

Chapter V.

THE CLOSING OF THE INDIAN MINTS.

By far the most important phase of the Silver crisis has been the closing of the Indian Mints, and the stroke of the pen which decreed that the public should no longer be permitted to convert silver bullion into coined rupees, has introduced the greatest currency revolution the world has probably ever seen. It has already been pointed out that the depreciation of silver has worked no evil effects upon the native population of that great Empire, and in most respects a silver currency is eminently more suitable for it than a gold one. The vast populations of both India and China are sunk deep down in poverty, and in general the possession of monetary wealth is of the scantiest. The great bulk of the transactions are for such small amounts that the copper anna rather than the silver rupee is quite adequate for their settlement. Under the natural order of things, therefore, the circulating medium would be of inferior value compared with that of the wealthier West.

But the losses incurred by the Anglo-Indian Government officials, the deficiencies in the Indian Budget owing to the constant decline in exchange, and the risks run by the commercial community in their relations with gold standard countries, brought about an agitation which, under the name of the Indian Currency Association, sought to introduce into India a gold standard, and thus abolish all fluctuations in exchange between England and her great Eastern possession. Under ordinary circumstances the agitation would have been ignored by the Home Government, but, unfortunately, it was strongly, almost violently, supported by all the officials responsible for the finances of India, from the Viceroy downwards, and the British Cabinet was compelled to give it attention. Silver had fallen to below three shillings an ounce, and the exchange to something under one shilling and threepence the rupee. The agitation for the repeal of the Sherman Act in the United States was at its height, and the opinion was general that, the moment repeal became an accomplished fact, the metal would experience a further severe fall. It was declared that under such circumstances India was confronted by the most serious outlook, and that the decline in the value of the rupee to a shilling or less would mean nothing short of national bankruptcy.

Such deliberate statements from men of such ability and high authority dared not be treated with contempt, and the outcome was the now famous Herschell Committee.

The Closing of the Indian Mints. 47

The members of this Committee were all men of the greatest financial knowledge, as well as sound economists, and could be relied upon to arrive at a decision free from all personal prejudice. They sought evidence in all quarters, and no doubt paid special attention to those who advocated a gold standard without a gold currency. The two great examples of this were our own possession of Canada and the Dutch possession of Java, in the former of which the silver dollar is the medium of circulation, and yet, in commercial transactions with England, is always calculated at the gold rate of exchange; and in the latter the silver florin circulates with equal freedom both in Java and Holland. But Canada is in close proximity to, and has large commercial transactions with, the United States, and trade balances between the colony and mother country, which would ordinarily require settlement in bullion, are almost invariably arranged through the medium of New York, where all the great Canadian banks have important branches. Java, too, although having thirty millions of inhabitants, and doing a large foreign trade, has the advantage of the protection of a wealthy European gold standard country, and any trade balances which require to be settled with a foreign customer, who would naturally object to receive depreciated silver coin, are arranged through

Amsterdam, where the credit of their most important colony is regarded with as much jealousy as their own. The comparison of either, therefore, with our great Indian Empire, containing two hundred and thirty millions of inhabitants, and with an annual foreign trade estimated at two hundred millions sterling, is somewhat unreasonable, particularly as trade balances with this country alone sometimes run to upwards of ten millions sterling in the course of a single year.

Clearly, however, the evidence on this point was considered weighty, if not conclusive; and the final decision to recommend the fixing of the exchange value of the rupee at one shilling and fourpence, and to forthwith close the Mints against any further coinage on behalf of the public, was based upon the belief that a settled rate of exchange could be maintained, and any further depreciation of silver rendered null and void as far as India was concerned. This decision, which, like most other State secrets, leaked out before it was officially made public, took most people by surprise, and those who knew the members of the present Cabinet to be thoroughly sound in their economical principles, refused to believe that they would ever adopt any such revolutionary measure. Although it has only been in operation a few months, failure is already stamped upon it, and there are not a few who, in pointing to the muddle which has followed, are inclined to urge that all the blame for it should be laid upon the Home Government. But a little consideration will show the gross injustice of any such proceeding. Many, if not, indeed, all the members of the Cabinet, must have doubted the wisdom of the measure when they gave their sanction to it. But the alarmist rumours, and the persistent prophecies of the evil which would result, which emanated from the Indian Treasury officials, really left them no alternative. The passing of the Sherman Repeal Act did bring about a panic in silver, which reduced the intrinsic value of the rupee to one shilling. Suppose for a moment, the British Government had refused their assent to the measure, and the predicted panic in Indian finance and Indian commerce had taken place, the entire blame for it would have been laid at their door, and there would have been an outcry that everything had been foreshadowed, and yet no precautions taken to prevent the disaster. The national indignation would have been so strong as to sweep them from office for a gross dereliction of duty, and no argument would have been able to convince the public that they acted for the best. They were really between Scylla and Charybdis, and acted upon the principle that of two evils it was advisable to choose the lesser. Had they acted merely for the object of clinging to office, our condemnation could not be too severe; but it must be remembered that the dangers of non-intervention were very real, and that, while they may have been doubtful of the success of the measure they adopted, they clearly foresaw the disaster which might follow a policy of absolute non-interference.

The natural outcome of this decision was a severance of the value of the rupee compared with silver. The former was fixed at an exchange of fifteen to the £ sterling, equal to one shilling and fourpence the rupee; the value of the latter it was impossible any longer to estimate, particularly as one of the principal outlets for it was now closed. The very definite rumours circulated as to the intentions of the Government had in the meanwhile caused an immense demand for the metal on the part of the great Anglo-Indian Banks, anxious to deposit as much as possible with the Mints before they were finally closed to the public, and its value had accordingly been artificially maintained. The edict announcing the decision was promulgated at a time when silver to the value of several hundred thousand pounds was in transit to India for this purpose, and the refusal of the authorities to accept it upon arrival led to a bitter and prolonged dispute between the Government and the Banks, resulting in a compromise, by which the latter were heavy losers. For the same reason the demand for India Council Drafts was enormous, and large amounts were daily allotted at rates advancing rapidly from 1s. 2⅜d., below which all applications had previously been refused, right up to 1s. 4d.

As usual, a foreseen event had been more than discounted, and remittances both in silver and Council Bills had been overdone, with the consequence that the demand for the latter at once ceased. A new and uncalculated upon event had also occurred. The sudden rise in exchange had stimulated the Lancashire Cotton trade, and, coming at a time when stocks of goods in India had fallen to an unusually low level, a business was let loose almost if not entirely unprecedented. As under any circumstances the India Council was always likely in the future to be a ready seller of its bills at 1s. 4d., Manchester shippers offered their exchange largely at something less, and this supply coming at a time when the export trade of India was at its minimum, and the demand for outward remittances consequently at the lowest point, put a total stoppage to the further disposal of Council Bills, which were unavailable except at a small fraction below 1s. 4d. The sales prior to the closing of the Mints, however, had been so immense, that for a time the finances of India were in no wise affected, and the Treasury officials regarded the matter with indifference, feeling convinced that, when the busy export season arrived, about November or December, they would readily obtain their rate, and that in view of the fact that silver was no longer an available means of remittance, they would have not the slightest difficulty in disposing of all the Exchange they wished on their own terms. But time passed, and matters did not mend. The pressure of Exchange from Manchester shippers continued, while the export season threatened to be late as well as poor. The demands of the Council became urgent as the balances in their hands rapidly disappeared, and as a temporary expedient, but strongly against the advice of the Treasury officials in India, an announcement was made that Bills would be sold at anything over 1s. 3¼d. Such a declaration defeated its own object, as it at once dispelled the illusion that the rate of 1s. 4d. was an absolute fixture, and that it was in the power of the Government to control the Exchange. More stringent measures even than the closing of the Mints would have to be adopted, and as competing shipments of silver had by no means ceased, rumour was loud as to the determination of the Government to impose an import duty on that metal. This only made matters worse. Silver experienced another speculative wave, this time started by the Native dealers in the Indian bazaars, who were eager to lay in a stock of the metal before the duty enhanced its value on that side. The large shipments to meet this new demand proved the finishing stroke to the tottering Exchange, and all faith in the maintenance of a fixed rate disappeared.

The rate of 1s. $3\frac{1}{4}$d. proved as unattractive as that of 1s. 4d. had previously been, and the Indian Government was confronted with just that financial crisis which the closing of the Mints was designed to avert. The competition of private drawers and shippers of bullion prevented the Council in London from obtaining the means of meeting its regular and heavy engagements, while the lock up of money in the Treasuries of Calcutta and Bombay, consequent upon inability to put it into circulation through payments of the London Drafts sold to the Banks, created a scarcity in the open markets of those great trading centres, and forced the Bank rate of interest up to ten per cent.

Thus every precaution taken to overcome the danger threatened to India by the repeal of the Sherman Act had been defeated, all the fond hopes of the gold standard party destroyed, and their prophecies falsified. The threatened bankruptcy loomed near, despite all their efforts, and the only means of salvation was a gold loan, issued in this country for £10,000,000, to supply the Council with funds, which should have been obtained by the regular sale of Bills. As the annual requirements, however, are something over £15,000,000, it followed that that process could not be repeated very often, and despite the frantic outcry of the members of the Indian Currency Association, the Home Government, through the Secretary of State, announced that in future no minimum would be enforced, and that sales would be made on the same principles which had always hitherto guided the Council.

Silver having fallen to 27 pence per ounce, which would make the rupee worth really less than elevenpence, while its exchange value is still in the neighbourhood of one shilling and twopence, it will probably be claimed that the closing of the Mints has at least somewhat minimised the disaster. It remains an open question, however, whether, if the Indian Mints had never been closed, silver would ever have fallen so low; nor is there any guarantee that Government interference, having failed to keep the rupee at 1s. 4d., can prevent it falling eventually to 1s. or below.

We have already seen the results of the policy as so far developed. It may perhaps be worth while to speculate a little upon what it may lead to in the future.

Allusion has already been made to the fact that the depreciation of silver has not in any way interfered with the progress of the native population. All its evil consequences have fallen upon the British official classes, and bankers, merchants, and traders engaged in foreign commerce. The grievances of the officials were partially redressed, and very justly so, by the undertaking given on the part of the Government to pay a certain portion of their salaries to their order in England at the fixed rate of 1s. 6d. per rupee, if they desired it, and so the loss incurred in remitting home for the education of their children and such like purposes has been to a great extent made good to them. But, granting that a fixed rate of exchange brought about by the closing of the Mints, and even a gold standard if it can be effected, will prove beneficial to the classes named, are there no drawbacks which infinitely counterbalance any such advantages? For, after all, we profess to govern India for the benefit of its inhabitants, and not of ourselves, although whatever tends to their prosperity must effectually benefit this country likewise. So far the natives have felt no ill effects from the new departure; but when it is borne in mind that silver ornaments form no inconsiderable portion of their hard-earned savings against a rainy day, and that the value of these has been reduced by at least twenty per cent., the matter becomes indeed a serious one. True, these ornaments are to some extent coined rupees, which have, consequently, not depreciated, but the value of the uncoined silver must be enormous, although there is no means of arriving at any fair estimate of it. And the question also arises—What has become of all the silver shipped to India since the closing of the Mints, the extent of which has caused such universal surprise? Perhaps some explanation may be forthcoming when it is remembered that, to the vast majority of the natives, rupees and silver mean the same thing, and they have not the faintest suspicion that the one has been divorced from the other. Here is a veritable gold mine for the shrewd and unprincipled trader, who can secure from the ignorant ryot coined rupees in exchange for an equal weight of the uncoined metal, and it is quite possible that, in the course of a few years, no inconsiderable portion of the vast hoards of rupees may in this manner have changed hands. While seasons are prosperous and crops abundant no serious results need be feared; but what may happen should famine once more overtake the land—as, despite every human precaution, may some day occur—is almost too serious to contemplate. It is then that treasure is parted with for food; that the bangles, anklets, necklaces, and buried bullion is reluctantly bargained away to maintain existence. Hitherto the metal has only had to be sent to the mint to be exchanged for an almost equal weight of rupees; in future, the natives must accept the best price they can obtain for a depreciated commodity, which is being everywhere pressed for sale. It is only then that the vast population of our great Eastern Empire will awake to the enormity of the injustice which has been done them. Despite the fact that, on the whole, we govern India well, there are always discontented but educated natives ready to encourage a feeling of disaffection, and to fan into a flame any smouldering symptoms of revolt, and any policy which would strike the minds of the people as one of spoliation might easily, in a time of distress, provide us with a repetition of all the horrors of another Indian Mutiny.

It may be said that such a picture is painted with unduly alarmist colours, that our hold of India is too firm for it to be shaken loose, and that if such a period as that described should ever arise, the Government could adopt extraordinary measures to meet it. But officialdom is slow to move, and history proves that the disaster has often overwhelmed those who were responsible for it before their eyes had been opened to the fact of its even threatening.

But we need not peer into the dim future for the evil influences of the recent fiscal change. Some of them are already apparent. The agricultural industry, which is the backbone of the prosperity of the country, is already seriously threatened by the competition of China and other countries which maintain silver as the basis of their currency. Just as the decline in silver compared with gold has handicapped the farmer in the gold standard countries, so the decline in silver compared with the exchange value of the rupee must handicap the Indian ryot against his China competitor in every article produced in both countries. In such important commodities as tea and rice, the difference between the real value of silver and the nominal value of the rupee will be a bounty to the China grower, and India, which has brought down the prices of produce to what in Western countries is starvation point, will now in her turn be starved out by others; while what may happen to the unfortunate European and American should China and Japan attempt to grow cereals or cotton on a large scale, can be better imagined than described. Such consequences will not happen in a month, but as surely as night follows day, so surely will the events prophesied follow one another. An immense stimulus will be given to production in every silver-using country, which must be followed by an even more severe period of depreciation than we have yet witnessed.

The expectation that the closing of the Mints would save the unpleasant necessity of imposing fresh taxation upon India, which she can ill bear, has been disappointed. The Indian Budget for the coming year is expected to show a deficit of about £3,000,000, to meet which a duty of 5 % has been imposed upon all imports with the solitary exceptions of gold, and cotton goods. As this only covers half the amount, and a strong agitation is being carried on in India against the exclusion of the last named article, it is more than likely that the tax will have to be extended to it, at the same time imposing an excise duty upon all native manufactures to avoid the cry against protection, which would at once be raised in Lancashire. Serious though this may be, it is infinitely better to boldly face and provide for present difficulties than to pile up disaster for the future, and a policy of rigid economy and careful finance must be at once adopted, to prepare for any further contingencies.

The exchange value of the rupee is at present nearly threepence more than the intrinsic value of the silver it contains. This is at a time when the export season is at its height, and the bulk of the import trade has been provided for. What chance is there of the maintenance of this difference when a few months hence the shipping season is over, and the demand for remittance to India consequently light, and at the same time, with a favourable monsoon, large forward contracts are being made for cotton goods, for which the outward exchange must be sold. The tendency of this difference is already to narrow, it may eventually almost entirely disappear. Should it do so, an opportunity would present itself for a reversal of the policy which has already proved such a failure. Governments, like individuals, are loth to include this word in their vocabulary, but the present one may be the less disinclined to admit it, because it is doubtful if they ever anticipated success. No serious harm has been done yet, but it should prove a lesson for all time against meddling with the old established currency of a great, and at the same time, ignorant people. Once the difference between silver and the rupee falls to a penny, it is to be hoped the Government will promptly throw open the Mints to the free public coinage of silver, and so allow India to pursue in peace her prosperous career.

Chapter VI.

REMEDIES: NATURAL AND ARTIFICIAL.

We have now dealt with the principal influences which have been operating on silver for the last twenty years. The great movements in the United States for maintaining its value have hopelessly broken down, and the net result has been the discrediting of the metal, and the attempt on the part of a great Empire, whose currency has been based upon it, to entirely demonetize it. There is much wild talk about the depths to which the value of silver may descend, and predictions are not wanting that at no distant period it will, like the baser metals, be quoted by the ton instead of the ounce. All this, however, is sheer nonsense; silver will continue for the remainder of this century, and likely for the next as well, to be the basis for the greater part of the world's currency; and counter influences are even now at work tending to bring about a speedy reaction, which it is to be hoped will not prove too violent.

First and foremost is the question of the cost of production. Scientific discovery and human ingenuity have between them cheapened that of silver, as of almost every other commodity; but there can be little doubt that at 27d. an ounce it is below the *average* price which it costs to obtain. There may be some mines which still yield a handsome profit; the Broken Hill Proprietary Company of Australia, for instance, is said to be able to market it at 18d. and realize a profit; and in such cases reduced price only stimulates the output, in order that the returns may be maintained. But there are few mines in either the United States or Mexico—which, between them, yield between one-half and two-thirds of the world's supply—which can live at such a price; and although many have struggled on during the decline in the hope of better times, they have of late been closing down on all sides; and it must be remembered when once this happens, the deterioration of plant and the displacement of labour is so serious that it will require very strong inducement and much expenditure of fresh capital to re-open them. The effects of this are not yet apparent. Ores which have been raised will be smelted, and accumulated stocks of silver will be marketed, and so, for the time being, there will seem to be little diminution in the supply. There has, however, been just a taste of the effect upon Mexico. All silver exported from that country is in the form of the well-known Mexican dollar, the Government obtaining no inconsiderable portion of its revenue from the seigniorage charged for coining. These dollars are shipped to the

East, where they are really the currency of great trading communities, like the Straits Settlements, which do not coin their own money, and largely even in China, and they are consequently in constant demand. They are intrinsically worth one penny per ounce less than the value of fine silver according to the London standard, but, owing to the falling off in the supply, they are now in demand at about a halfpenny an ounce more. Already, therefore, the fall in silver has put a premium upon the Mexican dollar of fully 5 per cent., although the market for them is free and open; and should this premium show any tendency to increase, some steps will no doubt be taken to coin a dollar outside of Mexico, and where there will be no seigniorage, in order to meet the demand which it is now difficult to satisfy.

Of course it must not be forgotten that one great outlet for silver has been closed, and that the repeal of the Sherman Act has suddenly cut off the demand for 54 million ounces, or about one-third of the total supply, which has been estimated of late at something over 150 million ounces per annum. The closing of the Indian Mints, if continued, must also sooner or later have an important influence, although, for reasons already alluded to, the shipments of the metal to our great possession have since that policy was adopted exceeded rather than fallen below the average of other years. We may calculate upon a lessening of demand from these two sources of perhaps 70 or 80 million ounces per annum, and the question then naturally arises, although it is impossible to answer it, how much of the 150 million ounces will continue to be produced, and how much of it can be produced without loss. Experience has also proved that the cheaper an article becomes the more uses there are for it, and it may be safely reckoned that there will be a great increase in the use of silver in the Arts. The future of silver, therefore, seems to be to a large extent involved in the question of supply and demand; and while it is unsafe to prophesy, there is reasonable ground for assuming that, the reduction of the one being likely to prove greater than that of the other, the natural tendency will sooner or later be for a rise in value.

There are many people who object to the use of the term "depreciation of silver," and who maintain it ought to be really "appreciation of gold." Both are right, for the baneful influences of the over-production of silver during the past ten years have been intensified by the continued falling off in that of gold. This, too, has happened at a time when there has been a veritable scramble for the more precious metal. Converts are notoriously bigots, and the European nations which have during the past twenty years adopted the gold standard have become enthusiasts in its favour. Political unrest has made every Continental Government desirous of accumulating a gigantic war chest, and the quantity of gold actually free for the conducting of the world's vast commerce is alarmingly small, and almost entirely under the control of our own Bank of England. Even Russia, although not requiring gold for currency purposes, is perfectly well aware that without it she would be placed at a great disadvantage compared with the other European nations, and has consequently accumulated and hoarded great masses of the metal in view of future eventualities and possible political complications; and not even the terrible famine, experienced in that country two years ago, could induce her to part with any quantity. The Baring crisis indeed was hastened by Russia growing uneasy, and withdrawing large sums into the privacy of her own coffers; and the very fact of her being a silver standard nation has been a standing menace to the financial position of Europe generally, as she can only retain her hold on gold by hoarding it.

Probably it is no exaggeration to say that the war chests thus formed in Europe amount to at least £100,000,000 sterling in gold, withdrawn entirely from circulation, and absolutely useless for all purposes of trade and commerce. Such accumulations must eventually cease, even if only from sheer exhaustion and inability to go on, and there are many signs that the limit has been almost reached. There is some hope, therefore, that the annual production of gold will in future find its way into more legitimate channels, and that, instead of being uselessly hoarded, it will pass freely into circulation. This is happening, too, at a time when great gold discoveries are being made, and the output largely increased,—the supply from South Africa alone, which five or six years ago was not worth taking into consideration, being estimated this year to reach some £6,000,000 or £7,000,000.

Such an increase in the world's available supply of gold must directly counteract the effects of the superabundant supply of silver; and those who remember, or know by repute, the effects of the great gold discoveries in Australia and California some forty-five years ago, may be able to form an idea of the possibility of a period of inflation which even the competition of the East may be fruitless to check, and which indeed would almost certainly force up the value of silver with that of every other commodity.

Precisely the same effect would result from a great European war, which would let loose the immense accumulation of gold, and operate in the same way as entirely fresh supplies. The first result of any such calamity would doubtless be panic and disaster; but the terrible destruction which would ensue would require an equal amount of subsequent construction and renovation, stimulating trade and industry all over the world, while there would necessarily be fewer hands to perform the work.

There is a reasonable expectation, therefore, that we may be approaching the end of the period of depression, and that the increasing supplies of gold may prove a natural remedy to existing influences. Everyone must hope that the change will proceed from the peaceful efforts of industry, and not from the dire calamities of war and bloodshed.

It is not to be wondered at that the enormous and constantly recurring losses of the past few years should have largely increased the numbers of those who, becoming impatient of any improvement from natural causes, insist that some artificial expedients must be adopted. There never has been so general an interest taken in the so-called Silver Question as at present, and yet it is astonishing how many well-informed and shrewd people frankly confess they do not understand it. The fact of the matter is, the prolonged and somewhat embittered discussions between the mono-metallists on the one hand, and the bimetallists on the other, have tended to confuse the real issues, which are extremely simple, and those who have not followed them closely soon lose the thread.

There are many doctors, each one having some patent remedy of his own, although the great panacea is bimetallism—now a question of so much importance that a chapter must be specially devoted to it. To discuss the scores of minor suggestions, many of them almost too absurd to deserve any notice whatever, would necessitate a volume by itself; but it may be profitable to examine a few of them, if only to show their uselessness or impracticability.

Perhaps the simplest proposal is the withdrawal from circulation, in this and other countries, of all gold coins under the value of a sovereign or its equivalent, and at the same time increasing the legal tender of silver in England from £2 to £5. This plan, it is supposed, would necessitate the increased use of silver; but as every country except our own has an ample supply of the coined metal to meet any possible demand, its effect would be almost infinitesimal, as the withdrawal of the half-sovereign, and the consequent demand for whatever increased silver coinage was necessary in this country, would be a very slow process. Nor would the increase in the amount of legal tender do much to help it. As a matter of fact, large amounts in silver are paid and received daily. Tradesmen doing a large business amongst the working classes frequently accumulate it to the extent of £100 or more, and pass it without difficulty over the counters of their Banks, where in turn it is disposed of just as readily to large employers of labour for the purpose of paying wages. The only condition is that it shall be made up in £5 packages, with the name and address of the packer legibly written upon it, and in this form they are as readily disposed of as £5 Bank of England notes. On the other hand, although £2 is a legal tender, few people in an ordinary retail transaction of this amount ever dream of paying in silver, and in the rare events where even £5 was offered it would never be refused on the ground of illegality.

One of the suggestions offered at the Brussels Conference, and by a British representative, was that the nations of Europe should agree amongst themselves to purchase annually £5,000,000 worth of silver at a price not over 43 pence per ounce, which was the quotation then current, provided, and as long as, the United States would consent to continue the annual purchase of 54,000,000 ounces. A little rough certainly on the United States! Probably, at the next Conference on the question, the same gentleman, on behalf of an United Europe, might have been able to offer them storage accommodation.

Most of the plans, however, involve to a greater or lesser extent the joint use at some fixed ratio of the two metals. It has been seriously suggested to mint coins consisting of an amalgamation of both in some definite proportion. The life of such a mongrel would be short. As fast as issued they would be shipped to some country where the single standard of gold or silver was still in use, and melted down. The standard metal would be re-minted into current coin, and the other sold or re-exported as bullion; and by means of fluctuating exchanges, enterprising dealers would in some way or other make large and regular incomes at the expense of their respective Governments.

Another proposed method is by arrangement among a number of Governments—the more, of course, the better—to increase the silver coinage, by slow degrees, by £2 per head of the population, purchasing the silver for the purpose in monthly instalments, beginning at the current price, and advancing by, say, one farthing per ounce per month until an agreed-upon maximum, possibly 60d., had been reached. This, it is claimed, would almost imperceptibly accustom the various populations to an increased use of silver money, while, at the same time, the rise in value would be so gradual as not to cause any violent oscillations in trade. It is argued that if only England, France, Germany, and the United States combined for this purpose, the eventual absorption would be gigantic. And what is £2 per head? Not much, it is true, if every member of the community took his share of the burden. But how many of the inhabitants of all ages, even of England, ever have in their possession at one time as much as £2? If we knew it, only a very small proportion of the total; and, consequently, the burden would either have to be borne by a very few, or, more likely still, the coins would remain at the respective Mints. In addition to this, another difficulty would arise. In the vaults of the United States Treasury, at Washington, there is estimated to be lying, silver of the nominal value of £90,000,000. The Bank of France has upwards of £50,000,000, and the Imperial Bank of Germany over £20,000,000. Neither the Bank of England nor the British Government hold any, except what is needed for current requirements. Would each Government be content to increase its stock by £2 per head, irrespective of present holdings; or would they wish to insist that, in the first place, some equalisation should be attempted. If so, neither England nor Germany could be expected to enter into an agreement which would saddle them with the superfluous and unsaleable load of French and American silver. Even if this difficulty were overcome, what guarantee would exist that the requisite supplies of the metal would be obtainable at the monthly farthing advance? Speculation would anticipate at least twelve months ahead, and, instead of the slow and steady advance, the fluctuations would become more violent than ever. If the respective Governments were not called upon to make the monthly purchase except at the agreed upon price, any one of them, tired of the arrangement, could so manipulate the market as to prevent the necessity of fulfilling the contract. And lastly, is it at all reasonable to suppose that the United States, already brought to the verge of national bankruptcy by the accumulation of £90,000,000 of useless silver, would consent to increase it by another £150,000,000, which would be her probable proportion before the agreement was completed; or that France would dream of more than doubling an amount which she would now be willing to make a considerable sacrifice to get rid of?

The more such a proposal is examined the more impracticable it appears, nor can it be said that any of its competitors share a better fate. The idea of an international silver coinage circulating in all countries is, if anything, still worse, and the limited trial which it has received under the Latin Union has been sufficient to prove its failure. Much of the silver coin in the Bank of France to-day would be in circulation were it not for the enormous amount of Italian and Belgian money which passes current, and out of all proportion to the French coin to be found, at any rate, in the former country. The metallic money flows naturally from the poorer to the richer country, being replaced in the former by paper or other depreciated currency, and becoming an encumbrance in the latter. The only prop holding up the Latin Union to-day is the knowledge that Italy and Greece, and possibly Spain as well, would become bankrupt, if compelled to take back their depreciated silver lire, drachmæ, and pesetas, at their nominal value.

The fact is, any scheme necessitating an agreement to place an artificial value upon silver must eventually break down, and the only chance of helping it, apart from any indirect assistance it may receive from a great increase in the gold supply, is to provide for it some outlet into which it will naturally flow, while allowing its value to be fixed by the inexorable laws of supply and demand.

Chapter VII.

BIMETALLISM.

The theories of bimetallism are by no means of modern propounding. As they are now known to us, however, they may be said to have been introduced by M. Cornuschi and Mr. Seyd within the past twenty years. For a long time these two gentlemen and their handful of followers were regarded as little better than crackbrained enthusiasts, whose doctrines were too silly ever to become dangerous. The wonderful and woful fulfilment of many of their predictions roused people to pay them a little more attention, and to think that, after all, there might be something in their arguments. Their doctrines have made rapid progress since they have been taken up in Lancashire, where an idea is prevalent—based entirely, however, upon wrong premises, as we have already seen—that the depreciation of silver compared with gold has inflicted great injury upon the all important cotton industry.

Outside that county progress has been slow until quite recently, but the latest great wave of depression has enabled its devoted apostles to sweep into their folds masses of people engaged in other industries, and thousands who, a few years ago, would have ridiculed the doctrines as fanatical, now lend a willing ear to the new gospel. It is only another illustration of the fact that the heresy of yesterday may become the dogma of to-morrow, and that people burned as heretics in the past become the saints of the present age. We are beginning to ridicule much of the political economy of our forefathers as old-fashioned and out of date, and perhaps some of its doctrines are inapplicable to our modern developments. Nevertheless there are great truths underlying its foundations, which will remain truths in all ages, and cannot be departed from without serious disaster to the welfare of nations; and prominent amongst these are the laws regulating sound currency. The heresy of bimetallism, therefore, is no less a heresy because it has gained, and continues to gain, shoals of converts: and the fact that among them are men of splendid intellect and wide business experience, makes it all the more necessary to combat it with renewed vigour, and endeavour to undermine it before it works irreparable mischief.

It is unnecessary to examine closely the old theories of bimetallism. The best of them have been handed down to the present generation, and it will be quite sufficient to deal with the case as it is presented to our notice to-day, linked as it is to new ideas gained by more recent experience. The great argument of its supporters is that, under some such arrangement, gold and silver were maintained at something like a fixed ratio for the greater part of two hundred years, and France is specially singled out as having, almost unaided, maintained the basis of 15½ to 1 for a considerable part of this century. But the currency of France never was bimetallic. The most that can be said for it is that it was an interchangeable mono-metallism. It is true that France coined both gold and silver in the fixed ratio of 15½ to 1, but it was rarely called upon to coin both metals at the same time. The ratio has varied widely in different periods of the world's history, and that of 15½ to 1 is one of the many legacies of the great French Revolution. From the beginning to the middle of the present century but little gold was sent to the French Mints, and at the latter period, the troubles we are now passing through were beginning to threaten. France was then practically a silver standard country, and as she possessed little or no more gold to be exchanged for further supplies of silver, the ratio promised to become obsolete, and the depreciation of silver about to begin. Just in the nick of time the position was saved by the gold discoveries in Australia and California, and in the five years 1848-52 the great bulk of those wondrous additions to the world's wealth was marketed.

While gold can scarcely be said to have become as cheap as dirt, there is no doubt its value at that period fell enormously, because gold, like every other commodity, is subject to fluctuations. It may be quite true that an ounce will always bring 77s. 10d., but that 77s. 10d. is much more valuable at one time than another. We talk about wheat, cotton, sugar, coffee rising or falling in value. It is frequently nothing of the sort, but simply gold falling or rising. An excess in supply or consumption of any single article will usually regulate its price, but there have been times when almost every article of merchandise, irrespective of the laws of supply and demand, has risen or fallen sharply, and this has been solely owing to gold being in very large or unusually small supply. Such a time followed these gold discoveries, and the universal inflation which took place influenced almost every article of use or luxury. Silver shared in it, and the demand for the inferior metal grew apace. France happened then to be the only country possessed of any large available supply, for the whole of her currency was in silver, and could be readily exchanged for gold. At once gold began to flow into the French Mints, and the silver coinage to rapidly disappear, until in a few years small change even was becoming scarce. From being a silver standard country she was suddenly converted into a gold standard one. For the next twenty years no change worthy of note occurred. The production of gold fell off, but that of silver did not increase to a sufficient extent to disturb the existing ratio, and there was no sufficient inducement to exchange the one metal for the other on any huge scale. But at the conclusion of the Franco-German war, as we have already noticed, Germany determined to adopt a gold standard, and once more France, despite all her sufferings, offered the largest supply of available gold. German silver poured in to be exchanged for it, and in a shorter time perhaps than it took on the previous occasion to convert France from a silver to a gold standard country, she would have then been re-converted from gold to silver. National sentiment, even more than economic policy, determined the French Government to close their mints against the German silver; and had this not been done France would to-day have been a silver standard country, and a traveller might have scoured the land from Dunkirk to Nice without finding a single French gold coin in circulation. Probably such an event would have eased the fall of the metal—it certainly would not have prevented it. France, therefore, has always been either a gold or silver standard country—never both at the same time; and this fact demolishes the first important outwork of the bimetallic party.

Until quite recently bimetallists all hankered after

the standard of 15½ to 1, probably as being the last one fixed. But since silver has taken its last downward plunge, and fallen to a price which represents about 34 to 1, we hear less of the old ratio, and most supporters of the movement express themselves willing to adopt one more in accordance with established facts. This at once raises the question, Upon what principle is the ratio to be fixed? As the main object is to raise the price of silver out of its present depressed state, and so cause a universal rise in prices to something like a reasonable level—whatever that may be— any suggestion to fix it at 34 to 1 would of course be rejected with scorn, as that would at once tend to consolidate permanently what may, after all, be only a temporary disaster. And yet it is admitted that the danger of returning at once to the old standard would be as great, or even greater, than remaining where we are. Silver has been declining for twenty years, but, with the exception of the last two, no single year has witnessed any important fall. Prices of all other commodities have been declining slowly as well, and the general average is now far below that of the period alluded to. But a sudden doubling in the value of silver would double the value of most other things at the same time; and, desirable as it may be that we should witness a general revival, any such rapid movement must prove disastrous. Any sudden *great* rise in the value of silver would be more to be deprecated even than a further fall. It would unsettle trade, and again sweep away the basis for the safe conduct of our great Eastern commerce, to say nothing of the heavy losses which would be incurred on the inevitable subsequent reaction. Some at any rate of the present trade depression can be distinctly traced to the inflation of silver four years ago, which led to such wild and unjustifiable speculation. Had India at that period held great stocks of produce or of British goods, half her native dealers and merchants must have been ruined; as it was, that Empire had in consequence to pass through a commercial crisis such as it had not experienced since the days of the great Collie and City of Glasgow Bank failures fourteen years ago.

And yet it is absolutely necessary that in any bimetallic system some definite ratio must be fixed upon, which shall not be subject to any fluctuations. If $15\frac{1}{2}$ to 1 and 34 to 1 are both out of the question, is there anything between the two? Perhaps 20 to 1 or 24 to 1. But upon what grounds would such a proportion be despotically arrived at? Not upon the cost of production of silver, because that varies from 18d. upwards. Not upon the basis of existing coinage in the principal countries of the world, because that ranks from between 14 and 16; and yet any different ratio to that in use in the respective countries would render all existing silver coinage obsolete. The fact is, whether we care to admit it or not, that gold and silver are simply commodities like everything else, and subject to the ordinary laws of commodities. It is just as reasonable to propose that the price of tea should always be regulated by law with that of coffee, or that the value of cotton should bear a fixed ratio to that of wool, as to demand that a certain fixed weight of silver shall always be of equal value to another certain fixed weight of gold. All of them are largely dependent upon circumstances beyond human control, and it is no more unreasonable for a tea planter to expect that he can obtain as large a price per pound for his production when the world's crops have been suddenly doubled, than it is for the owner of a silver mine to think he can maintain the value of his production under similar circumstances. There are probably no two things in the world which have maintained a steady, relative, and unvarying value to one another for a hundred years; and yet we are asked to believe that the changes which have occurred during that period, and which have, to a greater or lesser extent, affected everything, have left two metals absolutely untouched; or that some arrangement can now be made which will defy all the changes of the next hundred years, if not of all time.

Even granting that some satisfactory method of

fixing the ratio could be arrived at, the real difficulties of the case would only then be commencing. For no bimetallic principle could be put into force unless assented to by most, if not all, the currency-using countries in the world, and such assent would have to be obtained by some form of international treaty. But the history of the world is the history of broken treaties, and there have been very few worth the paper they were written upon, even before the ink upon them was dry. It may be argued that bimetallism would be productive of such universal benefit, that, once established, there would be no desire to depart from it. But we have to deal with human nature as it is, and not as it ought to be, and if any one party to the agreement imagined it had a grievance, or thought it saw some distinct advantage to be gained in pursuing some other method, the temptation to break through it would be very strong. It is a well known axiom that a chain is only as strong as its weakest link, and the backsliding from any such treaty, of even the smallest and least important nationality, would prove a constant menace, if indeed it did not at once destroy the entire fabric. Nor would such a state of affairs be at all unlikely to occur. At one time or another nearly every nation in the world has had to go into, at any rate, temporary bankruptcy. Some are in that state at present, and it would be too much to expect that others will not some day follow. We know some of the expedients adopted when such a disaster occurs. Specie payments are suspended, Government printing presses set to work, and an inconvertible paper currency forcibly put into circulation, and protected by all manner of pains and penalties. How would a nation in such a plight, and a party to a bimetallic agreement, stand in relation to its partners? It would be pledged to coin gold and silver at a fixed ratio, and yet putting neither the one nor the other into circulation, and there is just a possibility of its claiming to pay its foreign debts in something which it had based upon its metallic currency, which might be practically worthless paper. There would be little profit in discussing the numerous methods by which an impoverished nation might obtain advantage to itself at the expense of its wealthier neighbours if bound to them by any monetary treaty. The one least likely to occur to anybody would probably be that adopted; and threats to leave the Union, and establish again a single standard, even if productive of no important advantage to the seceder, might easily become a most effective method of blackmailing, in the endeavours of an impoverished nation to raise a foreign loan.

The initial difficulties in forming any such union are, however, insuperable. Prejudice and sentiment play a greater part in the history and legislation of nations than we care to admit, and, rightly or wrongly, Europe now believes that the possession of gold is necessary not merely to commercial prosperity, but even to existence itself. Statesmen may be willing to attend congresses, and assist in academic discussions on the question; but wherever sacrifices have been made to accumulate gold, they have no intention of permitting the fruit to slip through their fingers. There may be weighty reasons why a bimetallic union should be formed, but there are still weightier ones why their particular country should either remain outside it altogether, or be accorded special privileges to induce it to enter. The United States have been endeavouring to support silver for fifteen years, and now naturally think some other nation should bear a greater share of the burden. France has already £50,000,000 of silver coin in the vaults of her National Bank, and fails to understand why she should be called upon to increase it in the same proportion as England, who has none; and finally, England, which has up to the present got on exceedingly well without any, has not yet been educated up to understand why she should encumber herself with what has proved such a white elephant to her neighbours. Nor are European countries the only ones to be considered. China, for instance, could have no object in becoming a partner in a bimetallic union, nor are the various Republics of South America at present in a position to do so, even did they wish it. But there is much private wealth in these countries, and in the hands, too, of people who have no doubt closely watched the tendency of modern fluctuations. They cannot fail to have noticed that gold is one of the very few things which of late years has maintained its value, and, sceptical of the miracle to be worked by bimetallism, they would absorb gold, wherever and whenever available, in exchange for silver or any other available commodity; and its first effects, therefore, would be a rapid disappearance of the more precious metal from the bimetallic countries, accompanied, very likely, by a renewed scare on the part of those who were losing it, and an eventual return to a single silver standard.

It is, on the other hand, not impossible that a bimetallic union, if it could be formed, might at first enjoy some measure of success. For some years there might be a great revival in trade, brought about by a greatly enlarged currency and a superabundance of money, general prosperity, and an apparent absence of any evil consequences. The bimetallist would point with exultation to the fulfilment of his most sanguine predictions, and the world would wonder why such a wise and beneficent system was not adopted years before. But the Nemesis of retribution would be slowly and surely approaching. Every known silver mine in the world, which could be worked at a profit with the certainty of obtaining a fixed price for its output, would be strained to its utmost capacity, and every unknown territory would be explored in the hope of finding new ones. Far-seeing men would hoard gold, the shrewd Asiatic would send his silver to Europe to be exchanged for it, and we should some day wake up to find we had been following a Will-o'-the-wisp, and that no inconsiderable portion of the wealth of the world had been transferred from the West to the East. True, we might be possessed of great heaps of what we were pleased to call money, as the African negro formerly possessed cowries, but what was really valuable would have gone elsewhere. We might discover, with Benjamin Franklin, only it is to be feared too late, that it is possible to pay too much for one's whistle.

Bimetallism can be summed up in two words, "Inadvisable," "Impracticable." Inadvisable, because what little experience we have had of anything approaching it, has proved its utter futility to accomplish a steady maintenance of the value of silver, or to prevent a general fall in prices. What has happened in the United States, as the result of silver legislation, is only what would happen sooner or later on a much larger scale in any country or countries which adopted it. The production of silver has been stimulated beyond all reasonable requirements, and has become an incubus to the Western World, although certainly helping to materially increase the wealth of the Eastern. There is ample room there for progress in that as in almost every other direction; and with the spread of modern civilization and the growth of intelligence, accompanied as they will be by new wants and demands for greater facilities of communication, China alone will have the power of absorbing wealth in the form of silver bullion to an extent which, with patience, will do something to relieve the existing pressure. This will not be the work of a day, and any policy calculated to encourage an excessive production of silver will only tend to defer the period of eventual deliverance.

Bimetallism is impracticable, because it would involve the absolute reliance of one nation upon the good faith of others. However desirable such a state of things may be, it would be simply self-deception to blink the fact that we are far from having attained it; and although every approach to our neighbours—whether by treaty or simple understanding—helps to remove prejudices and create a friendly feeling, the interests in this case are too vast to risk a merely philosophic or economic experiment which, were it to break down, would involve the world in the worst financial crisis it has ever known. Our commercial relations to each other are now regulated by treaties made for fixed periods, in order that, when the time has expired, both sides may reconsider their position and examine into the changes which have in the meantime occurred, tending to introduce new conditions; and the only agreements made for an indefinite time are those imposed by a strong nation upon a weak or defeated one. A bimetallic league once formed, its dissolution could only be the cause of widespread calamity, and it would be eminently unwise for any people to bind their successors by ties which could only be broken amidst distress on one side, and disaster on the other. The increasing horrors of war exercise a distinct tendency towards its prevention, and assist in frequently bringing about the settlement of disputes, which would in former days have been left to the arbitrament of the sword, in some more amicable manner. But it does not prevent the possibility of some future outbreak. It may be claimed that the consequences of any nation, once committed to a bimetallic union, breaking away from it, would be so serious as to prove in itself a sufficient preventative. But as in the one case, so in the other; the longer the opposing forces are kept apart, the more deadly will prove the conflict should it eventually take place. "Better bear the ills we have than fly to those we know not of."

Chapter VIII.

CLASS INTERESTS AND THE SILVER QUESTION.

The Battle of the Standards, as it has been appropriately named, has been waged chiefly by individuals and sections of the community who have had some personal interests at stake. Here and there the cudgels have been taken up from conviction, by men who have believed that the adoption of the views they advocated would prove beneficial to the community at large, without conferring any special benefit upon themselves. But until lately the question has been considered too abstruse and uninteresting to attract any but those who had an axe to grind, although, as a matter of fact, there is nothing at the present moment of such universal importance as some solution of this much vexed problem.

It is not difficult to discover excellent reasons why some of the leaders of the bimetallic movement so eagerly promulgate their views. Several of the United States Senators, for instance, are amongst the largest and wealthiest owners of silver mines in the world; and it would be indeed surprising if they failed to support, with all their energy, any movement calculated to put a stop to the continued depreciation of their property. Again, in States like Colorado and Nevada, although only a moderate percentage of the population may be actually engaged in the occupation of mining, most of the remainder is in some way or other dependent upon it. Machinery is required in the mines, stores have to be kept going to supply the workmen, railways constructed to carry the produce, and food grown to enable everyone to live. Thus almost every industry in such States is only a line radiating from the common centre of mining; and it is little to be wondered at that such communities are always ready to cast a solid vote in favour of any legislation tending to benefit silver. Left to themselves, they would have but little weight against the vast total of the population of the American Union. But every agriculturist feels, also, that he has a personal interest in the question. He bought his land, very likely, for a mere trifle, when in its virgin state, and borrowed money at a high rate of interest to clear and cultivate it. As long as prices were remunerative he paid his interest without a murmur, and lived comfortably on what was left. The competition of silver-using countries, however, has reduced the price of his produce to close upon, or perhaps even below, the cost of its production; while, at the same time, the demand of the bank or money-lender for the full rate of interest on his mortgage is inexorable.

He has now to sell everything he grows in exchange, practically, for depreciated silver, while all his old debts and interest have still to be discharged in the gold which he originally borrowed. He too, therefore, has thrown in his lot with the mine-owner and his dependents, and this is really the explanation of the immense following of the silver party in the United States. While checked for the time being, and appalled by the disasters which have overtaken their country, there is no guarantee that the agitation may not at any moment break out afresh, and the victory of the gold party prove, after all, but a temporary one.

On very similar grounds bimetallism is becoming extremely popular among the farmers in our own country. They, too, have suffered cruelly from the greatly reduced prices of agricultural produce, but beyond that the analogy with their American competitors hardly goes, as very few British farmers now cultivate their own freeholds, and rents which they have to pay in lieu of interest have been very generally reduced. The agitation, therefore, is hardly pursued with the same vigour; and the conservative instincts with which they are imbued tend to make them somewhat suspicious of such new-fangled doctrines, and to cast their hopes rather upon old-fashioned and better understood palliatives. For all that, some of the most trusted leaders of the agricultural interest on both sides of politics are avowed and enthusiastic bimetallists.

The motives of the cotton spinners and manufacturers of Lancashire have already been looked into, as well as those which have influenced the opinions of Indian Government officials and merchants engaged in Eastern trade. Many of the latter classes, who are supporters of the recent policy resulting in the closing of the Mints, are in reality warm and even enthusiastic advocates of bimetallic doctrines, and have only adhered to the gold standard in sheer despair of ever witnessing the adoption of their favourite theories.

We have seen, therefore, that the representative men of any important classes who advocate bimetallism are influenced by the desire of conferring some direct benefit upon those classes, and the offer of other effective remedies would likely tempt them from the path. We should certainly, in one sense at least, be losers; the flowery eloquence and bulky literature to which we are growing so accustomed would become dreams of the past.

But we must not for a moment allow ourselves to be carried away by the idea that while bimetallists are types of everything that is selfish, their opponents are all actuated by principles of pure philanthropy, and take their stand only upon the foundation of sound principles of political economy. No doubt the majority of those who approach the study of the question without previously formed prejudices will throw in their lot with the supporters of the single standard, either of silver or gold. But there are large numbers of people as interested personally in the maintenance of the single gold standard as the Silver Kings of Colorado are in the establishment of the double one. Bankers, and all corporations or individuals whose money is lent out at interest rather than invested, or sunk in trade or manufacturing enterprise, are deeply concerned in the continuation of the present state of affairs. The possessor of a hundred thousand sovereigns to-day is twice as rich a man as the possessor of the same amount a quarter of a century ago, because now that quantity of gold will purchase quite double what it would then. Every penny decline in silver, with its corresponding depreciation of most other commodities, makes the owner of every sovereign a relatively wealthier individual; and it is out of no overflowing affection for the best interests of humanity that bankers and the financial classes, with scarcely an exception, are determined opponents of bimetallism. A continued decline in silver will benefit them so long as it does not lead to wholesale bankruptcy, and even when that fatality ensues, the banker is generally found to be the best protected creditor. Some of them even advocate the entire demonetization of silver, and it is said of a well-known capitalist in the city of London, who is, at the same time, one of the most enthusiastic supporters of a universal gold currency, that whenever compelled to change a half sovereign, he is uneasy while the loose silver remains in his possession. The same spirit animates the great bankers and capitalists of every large city in Europe and America; and so openly do those of the latter continent express their views, that they have roused against themselves the hostility of nearly every debtor in it, and have gained for themselves the somewhat uncomplimentary synonym of "gold bugs."

Great corporations, whether municipal or industrial, which have to borrow, and are able to offer security of a solid and permanent character, have also largely benefitted by the present state of things, as they are now able to obtain money at a lower rate of interest than ever before. Consols now yielding $2\frac{3}{4}$ %, and in a few years to be reduced to $2\frac{1}{2}$, sell at the same price that the Three Per Cents. stood at a few years ago. The loans of our great cities and boroughs paying $3\frac{1}{2}$ per cent., and issued ten or fifteen years ago at something under par, now stand at premiums ranging from 10 up to nearly 20 per cent.; and so with all descriptions of gilt-edged securities, in consequence of which all new issues are made on more favourable terms than formerly. This result can be traced directly to the appreciation of gold, the £3 now obtainable being really of more value than the £4 or £4 10s. in byegone days.

That large class of individuals enjoying fixed incomes, derived from public appointments, pensions, salaries, or any similar sources, must also be placed among the beneficiaries of the change which has been going on, inasmuch as the fixed sum they annually draw will procure for them now much more of this world's goods than formerly, and every accentuation of the process is really an equivalent to an increase in income. The lower remuneration now offered for the services of, say, mercantile clerks, and which is supposed to be almost entirely due to an overcrowding of the market, and its resulting fiercer competition, is really in part only a reflection in the change which has taken place in the relative value of that remuneration compared with other things.

We have, therefore, wealthy and influential classes of the community in all civilized countries directly interested in maintaining a gold monopoly, and whose opposition to any legislation favourable to silver, or any other commodity which might enter into competition with gold, is based on grounds just as selfish as those of any of the United States Senators, whose action has lately been held up to public condemnation.

There are other classes not quite as directly, but still traceably, affected by the slow revolution which has been taking place. While we have seen possessors of fixed incomes benefitted by it, another section, and one with which much sympathy must be felt, has suffered more or less severely. Those deriving incomes from investments made under wills or trusts, have experienced a considerable diminution in them, owing to the reduced returns obtainable from almost every security in which it is legal for trust money to be placed. As this class is largely composed of widows, orphans, and those who from some mental or physical infirmity are unable to support themselves, many who have been accustomed to live in comparative affluence have been reduced to the verge of poverty, largely owing to the beggarly interest obtainable on their meagre capital. It is true the cost of living has also been proportionately reduced, but this reduction is almost confined to food and a few other necessaries, which, although forming the vast bulk of the world's production, by no means absorb a corresponding proportion of the world's expenditure. It is indeed astonishing to what a trifling extent the general fall in prices has affected the luxuries of life; and when we expostulate with the fashionable tailor, dressmaker, milliner, or dealer in fancy articles, whether for use or ornament, about the immobility of their charges, they have always some excellent reason why their particular branch of trade cannot afford to make reductions. As middle-class life is only tolerable when it can command something beyond the bare necessities of existence, it follows that the change which has taken place in the value of money presses with especial hardship upon large numbers occupying that station.

While the rate of interest has fallen so heavily on money secured on high-class permanent collateral, it has remained practically unchanged on a class of property which would be the most benefitted—real estate. It is not necessary here to go into the relative rights and duties pertaining to real and personal property; we must accept facts as we find them, and depreciation has been felt no more severely than by small land and property owners. With the terrible reduction in the value of everything produced on the land, it is only natural and just that rents should fall heavily; but this fall has extended to land and buildings of all descriptions, and for whatever purposes used, although there are, of course, exceptions to this rule brought about by special local environments. At a time, therefore, when a reduction of the permanent charges—particularly interest on money borrowed for improvements or necessary building extensions—is most needed, and would prove most beneficial, the burden remains as heavy as ever. The risk of depreciation is too great; lenders have found to their sorrow that security, valued at much more than they advanced years ago, can now only be realised at a material sacrifice, and they insist, therefore, upon a return which will compensate them for the possible future loss of a portion of their capital.

The further we examine into it the more evident does it become that the ramifications of the Silver Question have extended themselves deep down into our social system, as well as spread themselves everywhere over the surface. No greater mistake can be made than to suppose that it concerns only capitalists and financiers, and that they had better be left to fight the matter out. While it remains in their hands, no satisfactory settlement will ever be arrived at. The silver interest and the bimetallists may be powerful, but the gold interest and the mono-metallists are more than a match for them. Backed by tradition, social position, and incalculable wealth, their position is too strong to be even seriously shaken by their opponents. Unflinching and unyielding, they will resolutely refuse to give way an inch, lest it should be followed by the demand for an ell.

Every shipowner and merchant, every shopkeeper and artisan, has a deep interest in this question if he would only realise it; and the only chance of ever arriving at any definite arrangement is by shifting the battle-ground from its present confined arena to some larger plane, where everyone who wishes can take his part. The objects to be attained by three-fourths of the community are identical, and may be condensed in the now well-known phrase, "A fair day's wage for a fair day's work." If only once some method could be devised for attaining them, a combination of these interests would easily overcome the resistance of either silver kings or city bankers, or, if, necessary, both together. Whether any such method exists or can be invented may be an open question. Many more visionary objects have been pursued in our own generation; and at least no harm can be done in making some resolute attempt, and even running some little risk, provided any resulting loss is not irretrievable.

Chapter IX.

A NEW OUTLET FOR SILVER.

Europe is now indissolubly wedded to the gold standard, nor are the siren charms of her bimetallist wooers ever likely to induce her to forsake the path of interest, which is, at the same time, the path of duty. Asia is equally attached to the silver standard, nor will an edict issued from London ever succeed in changing at a stroke the manners and customs of a continent containing fully one-half of the world's inhabitants. The position of the United States is somewhat more doubtful. Twelve months ago that country was on the verge of being precipitated from a gold to a silver standard, and although the danger has for the time being passed away, former experience of the eccentricities of American legislators would make it unwise to predict that it will never return. What particular injury would be inflicted upon that country by the adoption of the silver standard it would not be easy to discover. Sentimentally, she might be classed among the poorer nations of the Eastern hemisphere, instead of among the richer ones of the Western, and that would hurt Yankee pride. Her great capitalists might find their possessions temporally reduced in value, and the currency in which their debts were repaid somewhat inferior to that which they originally lent. But as the currency they now demand is, if not actually superior, at any rate of greater value than what they lent, it would only mean shifting the loss from the shoulders of the larger debtor class on to those of the smaller creditor one. But then it is always regarded as a crime to offer less than was originally borrowed, although it is the essence of smart and successful business to be able to exact more than was originally lent.

These three continents, however, do not exhaust the world's surface, nor will they during the next quarter of a century occupy the greatest share of the world's attention. Africa promises to become the continent of the immediate future; but, inasmuch as her prosperity will largely depend upon gold discoveries, her currency will naturally be firmly established upon a gold basis. It is to the not less important and more developed continent of South America that our attention turns. The European emigration of the agricultural population, which has gone on so rapidly for so many years, has hitherto been directed to North America and Australasia. The tide now is being diverted. The United States will have no more of it. They have passed laws to make immigration difficult, and have inscribed upon their banner—" America for the Americans." Australian development has been too rapid, or rather the desire to found great cities has—in consequence of which she is passing through a crisis which will put a temporary check upon the growth of the population, as well as the necessity for it. The Republics of South America, particularly Argentina and Uruguay, where the climatic conditions are specially adapted for Europeans, have thrown open their gates, and offer unrivalled facilities to everyone not afraid of hard work.

The chapter recording the past financial history of these Republics is certainly not the pleasantest reading. The Baring crisis, with its attendant complete collapse of South American credit, occurred too recently, and its effects are still too severely felt to be quickly forgotten. The temptation to reckless extravagance on the part of anyone finding himself suddenly in possession of the means of gratifying every desire, is doubtless great, and may be excusable, but never when linked with calculating dishonesty. The boundless confidence exhibited by European investors in the progressive capabilities of South America, caused them to subscribe their money eagerly to nearly every scheme introduced, provided it bore the imprimature of some financial house of good standing. Many reckless ventures, with little chance of success, were thus promoted, and the money hopelessly lost. The worst feature of the case is that in too many instances the promoters themselves were well aware of this, and their only object was to secure the savings of a too credulous public. If possible, worse still, these men frequently occupied the very highest positions in official life, and made use of those positions for purely personal and selfish ends. The proceeds of many of the loans issued during this period were remitted to Buenos Ayres in gold bullion, largely for the purpose of floating new banks under Señor Pacheco's Free Banking Law, which allowed almost any individual to found a bank, and issue paper against gold deposited with the Government. The paper is now valueless, and remains; the gold is more valuable than ever, but has disappeared; and there is more than a suspicion that there are people in the Argentine Republic to-day who have an excellent idea of what became of it. The corruption of the former President and his associates was notorious; and they, at any rate, not only secured a large share of the plunder, but managed to retain it.

Although these men have been removed, and an honest Government established in their place, it proved a much more difficult matter to erase the consequences of their corruption and dishonesty. Notwithstanding that arrangements have been concluded with the foreign creditors, which are honourably adhered to, the internal finances of the country are far from being in a settled state. The currency, starting under the sunshine and the halo of a gold standard, has sunk below even a silver one, and now reclines in the shade of inconvertible and much depreciated paper, which, with very grim humour, is said to be based upon gold. The latter has practically disappeared from circulation, and even contracts made expressly payable in gold are liquidated in paper, and the premium taken into account; so that a debt of $100 gold would be discharged by a payment of $350 paper, gold being quoted at 250 premium. In this country, where gold is the standard, large payments are rarely made in coin. Established credit, and effective and rapid clearing, enable most transactions to be liquidated simply by cheque. Cash payments are sometimes insisted on, more especially in the case of solicitors, who would decline the cheque of a known millionaire against title-deeds of property. But if a payment of, say, only £1,000 must be made in cash, and gold were tendered against it, the receiver would probably think it was done out of spite, or to cause annoyance, and the ideal mode of discharging the liability would be two £500 notes. No such objectionable feeling would enter the mind of a Buenos Ayres lawyer under similar circumstances. His mouth would be much more likely made to water by the strange sight.

The Argentine Republic, however, is too intrinsically

rich to remain for ever under a cloud, and sooner or later there will be a glorious resurrection. With its finances still deeply involved, and distrust by no means entirely removed, that day may seem to be yet distant, and unless there is a fresh influx of capital the process must be slow and painful. Future prosperity must now depend upon agricultural development; capital must be expended upon such development before the fruits of it can be reaped, and the question arises, How can this desirable state of things be attained?

The first step to be taken must be to return to sound financial methods, and to bring about a full restoration of confidence; the Government must arrange with its internal as well as its external creditors, and provide for the eventual specie payment of its now inconvertible paper. To enable it to do so, a fresh supply of bullion will be required, and if the notes are to be redeemed in gold, Europe will be liable to a renewed drain and a fresh gold scare. But is it not possible to build up the future prosperity of Argentina, and indeed of every other South American State, upon the basis of a silver standard for their respective currencies?

Silver, as money, is every bit as good as gold if allowed to stand on its own merits. It is only when an attempt is made to fix its value upon some bimetallic system that it breaks down. In bulk it may be greater, and therefore not so convenient for large payments, but even in England, with its gold standard, coin enters to only a slight extent into our monetary transactions. Bank-notes, and even cheques, are not only used, but preferred, as they are always accepted with the knowledge that they can at any moment be converted into gold coin if desired. And yet there is no other country in the world where coin is so much used as in England. Our smallest bank-note being of Five pounds, most transactions below that amount are concluded in coin; but every other Government issues paper of smaller denomination; and where, as in the United States, dollar notes are largely in circulation, coin is not merely little used, but is positively unpopular. What is required, therefore, is not the actual coin, but the knowledge that it can always be had if required; and so accustomed have the people of the various South American States grown to the use of paper, that, whether the currency were gold or silver, notes would always be used in preference.

Nor would any injustice be done by the substitution of an actual silver for a nominal gold standard. The paper issue of the Argentine Government is supposed to be something under three hundred million dollars, while it is also liable under guarantee for a further enormous amount of bank-notes, issued by institutions which have defaulted. It would be obviously unjust to expect the Government to cash the whole of these notes at par. The greater amount of them have had a forced, and some of them even an illegal, issue at a large discount; and even when the nation has received and benefitted from the proceeds, it has had nothing like the face value. Were it, therefore, to offer payment in full in silver, even at its present depreciated value, it would be rendering itself liable for a great deal more than it ever received.

The position of the foreign creditor would remain unaltered, and all obligations incurred in gold would be met in the same metal. The fact of India and China being silver standard countries, has not prevented them making gold loans in Europe, and meeting honourably every engagement, despite the fall in silver and the consequent losses suffered in having to do so. Argentina would be much more favourably situated, inasmuch as she would commence her operations on the basis of cheap silver, while the others began theirs when silver was dear.

With the premium at so high a figure as 250, the task of resuming specie payments may, at first sight, seem an almost insuperable one. The premium, however, is a matter affecting the external rather than the internal trade of the country; and it matters little to the farmer or tradesman what it is, provided he can obtain for what he has to sell a price equivalent to that which he has to pay for his requirements. But the premium is a gold one, and were silver to be substituted as the standard, even were the metal at 30d. an ounce, it would be reduced by one-half, and resumption would not appear so hopeless with a specie premium of only 125. Prices, it is true, would fall heavily; but they would still remain at double those quoted in gold standard countries, and intrinsic values would be unchanged.

The programme may be a good one, but how is it to be carried out? The first necessity is ready money, of which the Argentine Government neither possesses nor has the immediate prospect of obtaining any. Besides, even if their credit stood higher than it does, the present depreciation and discredit of silver in all the markets of the world, where money can be raised, is such as to prevent the floating of any silver loan, and the only practicable method would be to borrow in gold and purchase the white metal on the market for remittance. But at present Europe is indisposed to lend any more to a State which only a short time ago seemed hopelessly and helplessly insolvent. Even granting that the men forming the Government are scrupulously honest and of undoubted ability, politics in South America are so uncertain that there is no guarantee that a few years hence a Government as corrupt as the Celman one may not once more obtain supreme power, and bring the country to the brink of ruin. Besides, the great financial houses, without whose aid it has hitherto been impossible to float any important foreign loan, would stand aloof; and any ordinary attempt made through other sources would, owing to their determined opposition to any form of silver legislation, meet with their secret, if not their openly avowed, hostility.

We live, however, in an age devoted to congresses, and have not only already witnessed more than one called for the consideration of the Silver Question, but are threatened with more. Suppose, instead, we had one called of all those interested in the trade and prosperity of South America, with a view to take some steps for their promotion. We have had meetings of bondholders expatiating on the follies of the past, and eager to appropriate every dollar of revenue, future as well as present, to meet engagements recklessly entered into. But is Argentina to stand still until she has compounded for all her past sins? It may not suit large holders of depreciated South American bonds to encourage fresh enterprises until all the old ones have been paid for, but by standing in the way of progress they are only delaying the time when it will be possible to do so. There is, again, room for the profitable employment of much outside capital, if some safe means could only be found for its introduction.

All the important banking institutions of Argentina have collapsed, and, despite many attempts, every effort to found a new and successful one upon their ashes has failed. No better opportunity ever offered for founding a great English-South American Bank. And why not make it the means of resuscitating the national finances, and at the same time establishing a sound currency based upon silver. One of the main difficulties in effecting such a desirable object, even under an honest Government, is the extreme jealousy on the part of the people of any foreign oversight or control. They are perhaps right; for when foreign controllers once arrive in a country, they are a long time in going, and the Argentine people might have vividly in mind the case of Egypt, which has now apparently passed permanently under British control. That it may be for the benefit of Egypt is altogether beside the question. A civilised people will always prefer its own democratic government, however tyrannical, to a foreign despotism, however wise and paternal. But the establishment of such a bank need give rise to no fears of any such interference in the internal affairs of the country, as its business would be to encourage trade and commerce, and not to interfere with matters of government. It must of course have a charter from the Government, granted for a number of years, be protected from any undue interference, and also possess the right to issue notes, strictly limited in proportion to its subscribed capital and its deposits of silver, or its equivalent in gold bullion. But, most important of all, it must be sufficiently strong in capital and management to inspire universal confidence. The directors must be men of the highest standing, and recognised business ability; and the capital sufficiently large to impress everybody with the magnitude and responsibility of the undertaking.

The notes of such an institution would naturally pass current at par, and would in this respect bring the Government issues into still further discredit. The inconvenience of two descriptions of paper money, the one inconvertible and at a discount, the other payable in specie and at par, would be great, and might lead to considerable frauds being practised on people who did not understand the difference between them; but in return for the concessions it received, the Bank would either have to lend or guarantee to float a loan, covered of course by some tangible security, sufficiently large to enable the Government to resume specie payments in silver. This perhaps appears a very large order, but no Government is ever called upon to meet all its notes at any one time, even if its solvency is more than suspected. At first there would be a rush to cash them, and a few million dollars would be withdrawn from the treasury; but once the public were satisfied they could get the cash in exchange for their notes on demand, there would no longer be any object in presenting them; and, circulating at par, they would be a much more convenient form of money than the coin, while the Government would have a chance of accumulating a handsome reserve.

Those responsible abroad for the management of such a bank would naturally be in a position to form a just idea of the requirements of the country; and where their own funds were insufficient, or the nature of the undertaking unsuitable for temporary banking accommodation, they might readily assist in raising capital of a more permanent character. There are financial houses in London to-day, whose names attached to the prospectus of a new undertaking, although they offer no guarantees, is a sufficient inducement to the public to subscribe to it blindfold; and there is no reason why loans or companies, backed by such an important institution, after fully satisfying itself both as to the honesty and capabilities of the enterprise, should not be received with favour by British investors, and thus prove the means of introducing much fresh capital into the country, to the benefit of everyone concerned.

The risks attending such an enterprise would doubtless be considerable. Its capital would have to be raised in gold and converted into silver, and there is always the fear that silver may go on declining. But where great issues are at stake, considerable risks are sometimes justifiable. So important was it to the commercial interests of the country at large in November, 1890, that the great house of Baring should not be suffered to collapse, that great capitalists and banks all over the country joined in a guarantee to the extent of many millions to avert the catastrophe. In doing so they ran considerable risk with no prospect of gain, as any surplus from the Baring estate must go to the partners. But in this case the chances of gain would be very great; and if, in addition to its legitimate banking profits, silver should rise in value through its operations, its shares might easily go to a high premium, and yield a handsome return to the investor.

Nor would the benefits be confined to those immediately concerned. If such a scheme were adopted, silver would no doubt rise in price; slowly perhaps, but surely, as the demand for it increased, and the present wide difference between the two precious metals would gradually narrow. But as silver, and not gold, would be money in South America, such a narrowing would mean there a depreciation of gold. Gold would be simply an article of commerce, and its declining price would induce people hoarding it to sell it for the currency of the country, just as they would their sugar, their wheat, or their cattle, if they believed those articles were likely to experience a drop. Gold would rapidly pass to those countries where silver could be obtained in exchange for it, and so the coffers of Europe and the United States would be repleted instead of diminished. The cry of scarcity of gold would no longer be heard, and France, Germany, and Russia, able to put their hands on a few millions whenever they chose to ask for it, would no longer retain with such a greedy grasp every coin and bar of which they can obtain possession. It is evident, therefore, that Europe has quite as much to gain as South America itself by the adoption of a silver standard for the currency of the latter continent. She must welcome rather than resent a demand which would relieve her of a portion of her heavy stocks of the white metal with which she is now encumbered, and might possibly be found much more ready to lend than she otherwise would be.

Were there any probability of such a change being effected, the first result would be a sharp rise in the value of silver itself. Terrified holders would no longer press their stocks on the market, and speculation would once more anticipate the increased demand for the metal. Such a result would of course partly defeat the object in view, as the present cheapness, as compared with gold, would be one of the strongest inducements for the adoption of the proposed new currency. But there need be no fear that silver would run away to any extravagant figure. The lessons of the past few years have been too recent and too costly to be forgotten all at once, and the increased demand would at first be only small. Those persons who would be commissioned to supply it could and would choose their own time for purchasing, and any attempts to rig the market would simply land the riggers with the stocks to carry until wanted, the supplies in the meantime, perhaps, being drawn from other sources. There is already sufficient silver in the world to supply all the requirements of South America for many years to come at a moderate price.

The £90,000,000 stored in the Treasury vaults at Washington will remain a constant menace to the stability of the metal. There is no guarantee that the United States may not some day, in a fit of repentance, reverse all their former policy, and offer the entire block in exchange for gold. True, there is a large note issue based upon it, but it is not that which keeps it at par, but simply the credit of the United

States Government itself, and the notes would pass as readily current were there not an ounce of silver left. What might happen under such circumstances is almost too fearful to contemplate. The last decline in silver from 30d. to 27d. per ounce is said to have been largely due to the forced sale of the Balmaceda silver lodged in the Bank of England during the Chilian Civil War. This did not reach £200,000 in value, and if such a quantity depresses the price 3d. an ounce, what would become of the market were £90,000,000 to be thrown upon it? But with such an outlet as South America open to them, the United States could have no object in acting in so insane a manner, as they could, in the course of time, dispose of a considerable—perhaps the entire—amount of their holding. Should the demand eventually reach such proportions that this supply, in addition to the annual output of the mines, proved insufficient, France and Germany between them could supply another £75,000,000, which they hold and have held for many years, and which they would only be too delighted to exchange into gold, not to mention what could be obtained from Italy, Spain, and Austria.

This matter has been discussed almost entirely in its relation to the Argentine Republic. Were the policy there to prove successful, Brazil, which presents many features entirely similar, would doubtless follow, and all the minor Republics would by force of circumstances be compelled in time to adopt the system of the greater ones; eventually South America would become as homogeneous in its support of the silver as Europe is now of the gold standard, and one would be as impossible to change as the other. Exchange between the two continents would be regulated by the price of silver as it is now between India and England, and would be no longer subjected to wild bourse and speculative operations.

With such an opening for silver it appears ridiculous to continue to attempt to force it down the throats and into the pockets of people and nations who do not want it. The scheme as presented here is necessarily but a skeleton, and requires flesh putting upon its bones. Skill and time combined may accomplish this, and effect such a decisive settlement of the difficulty, that, while the financial problem of the nineteenth century has been the depreciation of silver in its relation to gold, that of the twentieth may be the depreciation of gold in its relation to silver.

No settlement upon any such lines can ever be effected if left to the great financial and loan-issuing houses. Their interests are too much bound up in gold, and it must be taken in hand primarily by those interested in the commerce and development of South America, and assisted by all who wish to see the troublesome Silver Question out of the way.

Chapter X.

SILVER AND THE LABOUR QUESTION.

The Labour, like the Silver Question, has become of international importance, and although they may appear to be as far as the Poles asunder, there is nevertheless an invisible thread binding them very closely together. Whether we like it or not, the democracy is rapidly gaining the upper hand in this country, and many are the evil omens prophesied in consequence. Comparisons are made with former periods in history, say, for instance, the French Revolution of 1789, when such disasters occurred in consequence of the uprising of the uneducated masses of the people. The circumstances now are altogether different. Instead of an ignorant, down-trodden, and oppressed populace, finding itself raised suddenly to a giddy height of license and power, the process in England has been a gradual one, and while it has been going on, education has been leavening the mass. The idle vapourings of irresponsible, self-elected demagogues, meet with no response in the minds and hearts of the hard-working and industrious sections of the working class community, and yet there appears to be a continual conflict between capital and labour. Many would have us believe that it is entirely owing to the unreasonable demands of the workers, based upon an undying hostility to capital and employers of all classes; but the numerous instances of friendly feeling, and even of sacrifices made by the men for the benefit of their masters, compel us to look further afield for the real causes of difference. The leaders of the great Trades Unions are too shrewd and intelligent not to be aware that capital is the necessary complement of labour, and that, the one destroyed, the other would have little chance of existence. It is rather upon the issue of the fair division of profits that great industrial disputes are now generally fought.

It is a well-known fact that some of the noble families, and many of the wealthy ones in the kingdom, have acquired their position in days gone by through some trading or manufacturing industry, and the great fortunes thus made are frequently the boast of both speakers and writers when dealing with the magnificence of the British Empire. But while the employers were piling up their fortunes, what was being done for the workpeople? Living often in mere hovels entirely destitute of sanitary arrangements, with the barest and frequently no provision at all for the education of their children, working long hours for scant wages, they were left frequently with an entire absence of anything calculated to benefit their moral, mental, or even spiritual existence. It was the uprising against this state of affairs which led to the first and bitter conflicts between capital and labour.

Few people will be found nowadays bold enough to declare that the labourer is not entitled to share in the profits produced by his labour. The tendency is rather in the opposite direction, and to assert that a fair wage must be the first charge upon all industry. And by a fair wage is implied something more than sufficient to supply the bare necessaries of life. Education is now supplied free for the children, but there must be home comforts and an occasional luxury. It must be accompanied, too, by hours of labour which shall not exhaust all the physical strength of the labourer, but shall leave him capable of enjoying some reasonable recreation. Nor will many say that these demands are at all unjust; and in these days of the recognition of man's responsibility for the welfare of his fellow-man, employers of labour would themselves, with few exceptions, be the first to admit their justice. But the profits which would permit them to be not merely just, but even generous, are things of the past, and everything is reduced to so fine a point, that to make any profit at all it is sometimes necessary to squeeze it out of labour. The working classes do not, perhaps, sufficiently realise this, and look too much at the great and rapid fortunes made in former days. Nor can we greatly blame them when we remember that they constantly see around them signs of luxury and even extravagance provided by their own or their father's toil.

Much of the blame for this state of affairs must be laid at the door of silver. We have seen in a previous chapter how it has affected nearly every class of the community, and few more than the great manufacturing one, which has to provide for the wants of our foreign customers. They refuse to pay more in silver, now it has become depreciated, than they did when it brought its former value, and the difference has to be extracted from somebody. As the artisan refuses to give way unless absolutely compelled by force of circumstances—and wages often form no inconsiderable portion of the cost—the loss falling on the other parties interested becomes necessarily severe, and sometimes disastrous, and thus we get the terrible outcry of bad times. Once place employers in a position to make fair profits and they will not object to pay their workmen fair wages; and none will be more delighted than the workmen themselves to learn that their masters are obtaining a fair remuneration on their capital.

The labouring classes, therefore, have an enormous interest in the Silver Question, and should be eager to obtain a settlement. They are not slow to grasp any point which affects their well-being, and could the truth only be brought home to them, they would start an agitation which would quickly lead to something being done. The only fear is lest they should lend their support to quack remedies, which, while temporarily beneficial, would leave the last state worse than the first. We do not want the application of stimulants, which must be applied in constantly increasing doses to effect their object. We require some remedy which, however slowly it may work, is likely to effect a permanent cure in the end.

www.ingramcontent.com/pod-product-compliance
Lightning Source LLC
Chambersburg PA
CBHW031354160426
43196CB00007B/806